Interior of St. Machar's Cathedral.

(From old print.)

THE STORY OF
OLD ABERDEEN

BY
KATHERINE E. TRAIL

ABERDEEN: D. WYLLIE & SON.

1929

Arms of the Burgh of Old Aberdeen.

Dedication

To Brenda,

WITHOUT WHOSE HELP THIS BOOK WOULD NOT HAVE BEEN PRINTED.

ALL PROFITS WILL BE GIVEN

TO THE CATHEDRAL RESTORATION FUND.

FOREWORD.

THIS little book has been published in the hope that it will tell the story of an Ancient Burgh, which, owing to the relentless march of circumstances, has been incorporated in the neighbouring large town. The author hopes that it may interest the youth of Old Aberdeen, recall to many now far scattered the home of their childhood, and revive in the minds of those who are going down the hill the days of long ago when we had our own Provost and Town Council and were very proud of our independence.

It is a very simple statement, and does not attempt to answer any knotty points. If it succeeds in its purpose of interesting the younger generation, it will amply accomplish the wish of its author, who was born in Old Aberdeen, and has lived her whole life in the little place she loves so well.

She desires to acknowledge the very great help she has received from the late Mr. P. J. Anderson, from Miss Best and Dr. W. Douglas Simpson.

June, 1929.

CONTENTS.

LIST OF ILLUSTRATIONS.

OLD ABERDEEN

CHAPTER I.

FROM a very early date the burgh of Old Aberdeen, or Auld Aberdon, has stood upon the wooded height overlooking the Don, facing the waters of the North Sea on the East and protected on the West by the great woods of Forrester and Stocket Hills. The situation was well chosen; the river abounded in salmon and the woods were full of game. Both sea and forest afforded protection to the early settlers, to whom legend attributes the date of 3489 years after the Creation of the World! However that may be, tradition is busy again in the 6th Century, when we are told that St. Machar, sent out by St. Columba from Iona to found a church on the bank of a river which by its windings formed a shepherd's crook, decided that here he had found the place of which he was in search. He chose the high bank above the river where the Cathedral now stands; here St. Machar built the first little church, here he and his disciples settled, and here the Message of the Cross has been preached ever since. We know that St. Machar died in France in 594 after a visit to Rome, in the time of Gregory the Great. We have no idea who succeeded him, but we have every reason to believe that the missionary work was carried on.

Indeed, the fact that in 1136 David I., the "Sair Saint for Scotland," resolved to transfer to the church at Old Aberdon the Bishop's See from Mortlach, in Banffshire, would seem to prove that the Church and Mission had grown in importance. At the time of the transfer the settlement consisted of a "village of four ploughs," known as the Kirkton of Seaton. The charter of King David endowed the Bishopric with the whole village, a very large tract of country and the tithes of land, and money belonging to the King. The first Bishop of the newly created Cathedral was Nectanus, but what his church was like we have no idea. It became, however, the centre of religious life in the North-East of Scotland, and its power over the little community of Old Aberdeen was supreme, as its Bishops were at the head of its secular as well as its spiritual interests. Indeed, the Cathedral played so large a part in the affairs of Old Aberdeen that it requires a whole chapter to itself; but it may be interesting here to consider the buildings that housed the Bishop and his clergy in the immediate vicinity of the church.

Of these buildings there is hardly any trace now, but from the accounts given by Orem and Spalding we can form a fairly accurate idea of what they must have been.

We know that the Cathedral precincts were surrounded by a wall in which were four gates, the chief of which on the South opened into the Chanonry or direct access to the Cathedral. This gate was called Cluny's Gate, and was still standing in the beginning of the 18th century. Originally Cluny's Gate was surmounted by the effigy of the Virgin and the Arms of Old Aberdeen, while an inscription upon it ran :—

> "Hac ne vade via, nisi dixeris Ave Maria.
> Invenies veniam sic salutando Mariam."
>
> ["Pass not this way unless you say, 'Hail, Mary.'
> By such a salutation you will obtain pardon."]

At the Reformation, the effigy of the Virgin was destroyed, but the Arms of the city were still distinctly to be seen, and the gate was entire in 1725. Probably the gate took its name from the Laird of Cluny, whose house and garden, the most beautiful in the town, were just inside it. The name was preserved in the narrow road known as Cluny's Wynd, leading to Woodside, which has been swept away by the city improvements.

Another gate giving direct access to the North was on Tillydrone Hill, fairly near the top and close to the conical mound which tradition claims to have been heaped up by the nuns, who as penance for some sin were compelled to carry up the soil from the low ground of Seaton in their aprons.

The third gate was close to the little village of Seaton and opened into the Bishop's garden.

The fourth gate was at the end of the chaplainry, close to the chaplain's chambers. It was built by William Stewart, Bishop of Aberdeen, Chancellor of Scotland.

Like Cluny's Gate, it was standing in the 18th century. Within these gates were the Bishop's palace, the manses of the Prebends, the convent of the Holy Sisters of St. Katherine, and Bishop Dunbar's Hospital for Men.

Of all these buildings not a trace is left, but a short account of what we know of them from history and legend may prove of general interest.

The Bishop's palace stood a little to the north-east of the Cathedral. We are told that the palace was in the shape of a large court, having four towers, one at each corner. It contained one large hall and several rooms. An underground passage led from it to the Chancellor's house, of which only the outer wall still stands. The garden lay to the East, between the palace and the chaplain's chambers, of which the southern-most still stands in good condition, the steep roof with its crow's steps, and Bishop Dunbar's mitre, cut in the stone on the wall, giving us a clue to the date. The palace possessed also a summer house three stories high, from which a magnificent view of the sea could be obtained. In the centre of the courtyard was a deep well, and on the north side of the garden was a dovecot. The palace, judging by the inventory of the furniture and appointments, left by Bishop Gordon, 1577, the last Catholic Bishop, does not seem to have been quite worthy of its name. We are told that the wardrobe contained "five pairs of sheets one thereof sewed with silk, eight pillows great and small, two pairs of fustian blankets, one pair double woollen blankets and nine feather beds with bolsters; a great arras bed, with roof and head, with the King's Arms and Bishop Elphinstone's fringed; two arras

St. Machar's Cathedral, with Elphinstone's Tower.

beds with the same Bishop's Arms, a white Ireland plaid corset with black rings; an old counter cloth of Buchan weaving; a great press of oak and fir, a great long chest of oak; the pipes of an aqua vitae vat.

"In the chamber; one standing bed of oak, one long saddle seat of oak, one small counter, a portail.

"In the chapel chamber; one large oak bed with roof of arras and head fringe, an oak screen, an iron chandelier.

"In the great chamber; a large standing bed of oak, two counters, a long saddle seat, two forms of oak, a great portail, a brass chandelier suspended; eight small chandeliers, two iron fire racks, four cushions of needlework; the chamber hangings of sey, pale red, blue and yellow.

"In the closet; a standing bed of oak with curtains of sey, red, green and blue; a chair of ease, a small chair; a counter with cloth cover, a large saddle bed of oak, a cup almory of oak.

"In the study; a fire screen; an old saddle seat; a press of oak for breeches; a small oak chest for letters; a table for the crucifix; three boards with trestles and forms; a counter; a harthorn horse, a quhitstone chained with iron; an oak chair."

I have quoted the inventory in full, as it is interesting to compare it with what would be considered necessary for the furnishing of a Bishop's palace in our day.

Evidently this was the second palace on this site. The first was built in 1329 by Bishop Alexander Kininmonth, but was destroyed in 1336 by the English, who, according to Kennedy, "set fire to the burgh of Aberdeen." For more than one hundred years the Bishops occupied the palace on the island in the Bishop's Loch. In 1459 Bishop Thomas Spens rebuilt the palace in the Cathedral grounds, which was then the permanent residence of the Bishops till it, too, was demolished by the English in 1651, many of the stones being carried off to complete the fortifications on Castle Hill.

The Girth Cross, or Sanctuary Cross, stood on the Dovecot Green. William the Lion had ordered that every cathedral in Scotland should have such a sanctuary erected in its precincts. After the Reformation the Girth Cross was removed from the Cathedral and placed at the top of the High Street, where the Town House now stands. It was used as a Market Cross, and many allusions are made to it in the history of Old Aberdeen. At the top of the Cross was the figure of the Virgin Mary, destroyed in the days of the Reformation; below were the Royal Arms and those of Bishop Dunbar, Bishop Stewart and Bishop Gordon. Spalding tells us of a pretty Candlemas custom, when the bairns of the Old Town Grammar School carrying lighted candles marched round the Cross in a long procession "blithe eneuch." The leader, or Candlemas King, then climbed the Cross and fixed his blazing torch on the top. At the time when Spalding wrote the chosen leader was John Keith, brother of the Lord Marischal, and Spalding can only prophesy evil for the "dour Covenanter"; but we may be pardoned for

Bishop Dunbar's Hospital.

thinking of the joy that such an occasion brought to the children, whose lives must inevitably have been darkened by the times in which they lived. Not long ago the base of the Cross with the Arms of the Bishops was found in a neighbouring smithy, the hole for the Cross filled with scrap iron and rubbish. It is now preserved in the museum of King's College.

Very early mention is made of a Song School, which seems to have stood in close proximity to the Cathedral, but of which we have no exact information till 1642, when Dr. Guild, Principal of King's College, built a new school upon the site of the Bishop's Dovecot.

Another very interesting building stood near the Cathedral—the hospital founded by Bishop Gavin Dunbar, in 1531, for twelve poor men. It is described as "having twelve little chambers with as many little chimneys for a little fire in each of them." It had also a common hall and an oratory. It was intended by Bishop Dunbar to be a home for such men "as were of a good conversation," who had lived on the Bishop's lands or who had done work about the kirk, the Bishop's palace, Prebends' manses, or the Bridge of Dee. Failing these, old soldiers or blind or lame men might look to the hospital as an asylum. All the inmates had to be over sixty years of age; each man received twelve merks four times a year and a white coat annually. A very strict time-table was laid down. At 8 a.m. they must go to the oratory for their devotions, at 11 a.m. to mass in the Cathedral, at 3 p.m. devotions in the oratory, at 5 p.m. and again at 8 p.m. to devotions in the oratory. Dinner was served in the hall at one o'clock; each man had supper in his own room at eight o'clock. Exercises in the garden formed the day's diversion. No woman was ever to be seen in the hospital. The hospital stood to the west of the Cathedral in the grounds of Tillydrone until 1786, when it was handed over to James of Seaton in exchange for a house in Don Street, still called the Bede House. We have no evidence that this was ever inhabited by the Bedesmen. The endowment remains; eighteen old men receive 12/- monthly and a salmon a year from the fund known as the Bede, or Bead, Fund.

Close to the Cathedral in the Chanonry, or Chanry, were built the lodgings or manses of the Prebends. Each of these had its garden, "little taills," as Orem calls them. There were about twenty of these manses; the Prebends formed the Bishop's Chapter. They were parsons of country churches, but they had to live near the Cathedral that they might be ready to attend when required by the Bishop. That the manses in which they lived were not very large is shown not only by their total destruction but also by an inventory of the furniture each Prebend was expected to leave for his successor, viz. :—

"In the dining-hall: a large table, a silver spoon, a tablecloth and a towel. In the bedroom: a couch, a pair of linen sheets and two pairs of blankets. In the kitchen: an iron pot, an iron chain or kettle crook and a dish clout"!

We can very easily understand how much power was in the hands of the Bishop and his Chapter, living thus apart from and yet in the centre of the community, over which they ruled as Superiors, choosing the Provost, Baillies and Council.

CHAPTER II.

In a Charter dated 1498, James I. created the "Ville of Aberdon" into a "Free Burgh of Barony" with full power to its inhabitants to buy and sell wines, wax, cloth, woollen and linen, and to have and keep bakers, brewers, and butchers "as well of fleshes as of fisches" and other craftsmen. He decreed that every Monday should be Market Day and that two Fairs should be held annually—one on Skeir Thursday, that is the day before Good Friday, and another on St. Luke's Day, which was to last for eight days. The Skeir Thursday Fair must have faded away long ago, but St. Luke's Fair, or the Aulton Market, was, until quite recent years, the most ardently looked-forward-to day of the year by all the Old Aberdeen children. Two or three days before the market caravans began to arrive and take up their stances. Wonderful prodigies of Nature, such as the fat woman, the two-headed boy, and the boneless man, were exhibited; merry-go-rounds with their blaring music, cocoanut shies and rifle ranges were largely patronised by young and old; and the fun of the fair was fast and furious. The Aulton Market, too, is a thing of the past, but I am sure that old inhabitants have many a kindly recollection of it and the merry moments they spent there.

The Trades of Old Aberdeen consisted of hammermen (including smiths), wrights and coopers, tailors, shoemakers, weavers, and fleshers. They seem to have been quite flourishing; in the Town House are preserved some wooden chairs with the insignia of the Trades cut on their backs. The Trades were a source of revenue to the Cathedral, as they contributed half the entry money paid to them by the craftsmen. They helped also with the salary of the master of the Song School, and subscribed to the building of the new school. No craftsman could become a member of a trade without having first satisfied the deacon of his ability, and no person not a member of the Trade could make or sell goods in the city. So much for liberty in those days! The deacon convener was chosen by each of the Trades in turn. Early in their history we find them coming into collision with their brethren the Trades in Aberdeen. They decided to have nothing to do with the latter without special consent of the whole body; but this decision by no means ended the quarrel, which raged for many years. In their difficulties the Old Aberdeen Trades were greatly helped by Mr. John Paton of Grandhome and Mr. George Gordon of Rainnieshill. The gratitude of the Trades took what to us seems rather a curious, not to say depressing, form! One of the privileges of the Trades was to hire out mort cloths for funerals. Of these they possessed several of various qualities, the price varying with the quality. One was kept and lent gratis to any poor people who could not afford to pay. A minute of 1720 records that for the good services done by the afore-mentioned gentlemen, "the Convener and haill members of Court bind and oblidge them and their successors in Office that the sds. John

Paton and Mr. George Gordon, their wifes and children, when dead and unmarried, shall have the benefit and priviledge of the best mort cloathes belonging to the sds. Trades and that gratis, without paying any dues, therefore and this to be extended to the heir or heires of the sds. families in all tyme coming allenarly, gratis as said is." Aberdeen Trades continued to be most annoying, however. Old Aberdeen Trades petitioned Government to overthrow a decree of the Sheriff, as the members greatly feared that should the oppression from New Aberdeen be allowed to continue they " may at last bring us to be in no better caice than as if we were ther suburbs, as they are pleased to term us in ther vexatious process." Apparently Aberdeen ceased from troubling, and the Old Aberdeen Trades were allowed to carry on their callings peacefully. All the Trades had seats or " lofts " in the Cathedral; they were expected to attend service regularly and to accompany the convener to every funeral. A tax was levied for the " pretended Prince of Wales " in 1745, and this at a time when they were so hard pressed for money that they were obliged to resolve to give no more entertainments out of the funds. Recognising the very good work done by the Infirmary, however, a donation was unanimously voted for its funds. The Trades showed their generosity, too, by sending help to a poor weaver in Aberdeen who had been " burnt out." Surely this was heaping coals of fire on Aberdeen!

The Trades determined to do something for their women, and on some property they possessed in the

Chanonry they built a hospital to house ten women—either widows or spinsters in necessitous circumstances belonging to members of any of the Trades Guilds. The hospital was built in 1711, but apparently was not very popular, as we read in 1765 that the widows preferred to take the very small endowment and find their own homes. This did not appeal to the members of the Trades, as it does to us, and they decreed that the endowment would not be given to anyone not resident in the hospital, "it being to the loss of the house greatly to want possessors, who must burn fire therein." In 1792 the house was sold for £50 sterling. It is interesting to note that all the accounts are made out in sterling money from now on.

This Trades Hospital was the forerunner of Mitchell's Hospital in the Chanonry, better known as the Old Maids' Hospital. Founded in 1801 by David Mitchell, a native of Old Aberdeen, it was intended for five widows and five unmarried daughters of trade and merchant burgesses of Old Aberdeen. His intention was that the inmates should live a more or less communal life, be dressed alike in deep blue, and he would prefer that if possible they should all be of the families of Forbes or Mitchell. With a profound knowledge of human nature, Mr. Mitchell says, "As it is impossible to keep order and regularity among ten women except one of them have a superiority over the rest, I appoint the trustees to choose a sensible, discreet woman to be the Governess or Mistress of the Hospital, to whom all must promise due obedience." All who could earn a little either by spinning or knitting were expected to give half their earnings to the hospital, the other half they might keep for snuff or tobacco—surely a modern touch this! Strict rules as to diet were laid down. Boiled beef and greens were to be enjoyed for dinner three times a week, when the price of beef was not more than 4d. a pound; when it exceeded that, beef must be restricted to twice a week. Dinner on the remaining days was to consist of fish or eggs. One bottle of beer was allowed each inmate for dinner and supper except on salt fish days, when two extra bottles were to be divided among them all. Breakfast and supper consisted of porridge or sowens. The cooking was to be done by the inmates in turn, and Mr. Mitchell concludes his deed of benefaction by a pious hope that "the women would always behave in a Christian, decent and sisterly manner to each other and would be thankful to God for the quiet and comfort they enjoyed without being under the disagreeable necessity of supplicating these blessings from strangers or cruel-hearted relations." Something of a philosopher as well as a benefactor, this Mr. Mitchell. The hospital has still the same appearance as when it was built, but the internal arrangements have had to be entirely altered to suit the altered conditions of to-day. Four delightful homes, self-contained, fitted with bathrooms and electric light, are provided rent free to the widows and unmarried daughters of burgesses of Old Aberdeen. The spirit, if not the text, of Mr. Mitchell's benefaction is most carefully preserved, and the privilege of possessing such a home in these days of housing shortage is greatly appreciated by the lucky few. It would be well if others would imitate Mr. Mitchell's example.

There has always been a theory that the dwellers in the Chanonry were not quite the same as other people, a theory that was well illustrated when a stranger, asking the way to the Old Maids' Hospital, was told, "Oh, that's the hoosie in atween the twa daft Chairlies." The allusion was to Mr. Charles Burnett, who occupied 8 Chanonry, now belonging to the Botanic Garden, and to Mr. Charles Leslie, who lived in 11 Chanonry.

Mr. Charles Burnett, brother of the famous Laird of Kemnay, spent the latter years of his life in Old Aberdeen. Extraordinarily kind-hearted, he was a very good hater, and he had no regard for what anyone might say of him. He had a passion for flowers, and had he had a scientific training he might have done some very good work. He succeeded in producing a number of fine hybrids, but, unfortunately, was never able to account for them. His appearance was most picturesque, and he was a familiar figure in the Old Town, with his long silvery hair and beard and flowing Highland cloak. His brother, Erskine, lived at one time in Don Street. He shared the same love of Nature, and used to tell a tale of how, wandering in the woods one Sunday, he saw a kestrel's nest at the top of a tree. He did not think it right to take the eggs on a Sunday, so he quietly settled himself at the foot to wait for Monday morning. Immediately after midnight he climbed the tree and secured two eggs, which he placed in his mouth. Chilled by the long wait, he slipped coming down, fell heavily, broke his leg, and—what to him was far worse—the eggs also.

Opposite Mr. Burnett lived the Misses Gerard, daughters of Professor Gilbert Gerard, whose connection with Aberdeen and the Universities was a very close one. Their grandfather, Alexander Gerard, was Professor of Divinity in King's College, after having been one of the Regents in Marischal College. In his manse, the Chaplainry, he entertained Dr. Johnson and Boswell. In the Senatus Room of King's College are portraits of Professor Alexander Gerard, his wife, and Professor Gilbert Gerard. In the portraits of father and son we see a strong resemblance. Both faces are very gentle, sensitive and refined. Professor Alexander Gerard is also depicted in the famous caricature, the "Sapient Septem Viri." Gilbert Gerard was appointed Professor of Greek in 1790, and succeeded his father as Professor of Divinity in 1795. In 1803 he was appointed to the Second Charge of St. Machar's Cathedral. Pluralities were evidently permitted in those days, and doubtless he required all the income he could get for the upkeep of his large family of five sons and six daughters. The house, No. 6 Chanonry, was bought by his widow and inhabited by her and her daughters, none of whom married. The last two passed away only in the later years of the 19th Century. Old Aberdeen has often been compared to Cranford, and truly Misses Helen and Marjory Gerard might have stepped straight from the pages of that famous book. They had inherited literary tastes from father and grandfather, to whom also they owed very refined, sensitive, musical natures. The family love of being painted showed itself in them by their love of being photographed. They were always taken at a window, Helen holding the harp, which she played beautifully. The ladies lived a life absolutely apart from the life of the ordinary world. Their days were passed in semi-darkness, all the blinds were kept pulled down, and they never went outside in daylight. This peculiarity gave rise to much speculation, some people holding that they were Albinos. It was said that they had had a sort of sunstroke when crossing the Bridge of Don one April afternoon, after which they never again faced the sun's rays. Their dread of light was so great that they would sometimes go about the house under the shade of an umbrella or parasol. The close vicinity of the gymnasium rather troubled them, and forced them to take refuge in the back of their house. The atmosphere of their rooms was just like themselves, reminiscent of the days that are gone.

Absolutely different from the Misses Gerard were the Misses Forbes who lived at No. 10 Chanonry, up the long walk. They also were two delightful ladies of the old school, cultured and artistic, who spent their winters in Italy and brought home to the little Old Town a breath of a wider air.

Can anyone wonder that the influence of two such homes as those of the Misses Gerard and the Misses Forbes, combined with the culture and learning of the Professors, and the shrewd, kindly Scottish wit of the Misses Leslie, who lived at Powis House, must have permeated the whole of Old Aberdeen and have given some grounds for the feeling, so often expressed, that Old Aberdeen considered itself highly superior to New Aberdeen. Contact between the two towns was very slight. There were no means of communication, except by walking or hiring a cab. All the necessities of life could be bought or made in the Old Town; the large families of the ministers and professors, together with the boys of the gymnasium, formed a very happy community. Small wonder, then, that Old Aberdeen considered itself as a town apart, and less wonder that the inhabitants of New Aberdeen, looking at it with jealous eyes, made nasty remarks about the conceit and superiority of those who lived in "Sleepy Hollow." Well, well, these happy days are past, and no longer can the preacher pray, as Dr. Trail did in King's College Chapel, that a blessing might "rest upon this and the neighbouring city."

Of Dr. Jamieson in the manse, I suppose more stories have been told than of any other clergyman in the Church of Scotland. There was a spice of excitement about going to church when he was preaching, for one never knew what he would say, though one was quite certain it would not be what anyone else would have said! When Dr. Jamieson was in the manse, the Principal's house in the Chanonry was occupied by Principal Pirie. He, too, was not like other men, in that he had a bigger heart, a kindlier, quicker wit, than is given to most of the sons of men. His daughter is still with us, and it will be a black day for Old Aberdeen when Miss Pirie, beloved of all, high and low, for her great gifts of heart and mind, is taken away.

The Gymnasium, a most flourishing boarding school for boys, was also in the Chanonry. It was started by Dr. Anderson, better known as "Govie," whose extreme absence of mind was only rivalled by his kindness of heart. I think there is no doubt that the dwellers in the Chanonry, not so long ago, were not quite like other people, in that they were more original.

CHAPTER III.

BEHIND the Chanonry to the West was the Loch of Old Aberdeen. Probably the loch had been a peat moss, for we find that it was regularly let to various tenants. Water very likely collected in the hollows, for one of the tenants is to be allowed 6/8 for every animal that fell into the loch. Spalding gives us rather an interesting little touch when he says " that no maws or gulls were seen in the lochs of New or Old Aberdeen since the beginning of these troubles (1642-1645) and coming of soldiers to Aberdeen, who before flocked and clucked in so great abundance."

In 1662 James Gordon of Seaton drained the loch, and during the " space of his tack " he had plentiful crops of corn upon it. At the end of his lease the town took it into their own hands and rouped it annually.

We find many references to the loch in the Town Council minutes, which show us something of the life led by our ancestors. Washing day occasioned much trouble in Old Aberdeen then, as now! The water question was always a difficult one, and was a main argument for the union of New Aberdeen and Old Aberdeen in much later years. Springs in the fields to the west supplied a certain amount of water, and there were three public pumps — one in College Bounds, one at the foot of the Chaplainry Brae, and one in Chanonry just outside the churchyard! In addition, a small burn flowed from the loch, joined the Powis burn, crossed College Bounds, and so down University Road to the Links. It was evidently the custom to go out with washing tubs to the nearest point of the burn, there light one's fire, and proceed with the weekly wash. This custom much annoyed the Provost and Council, who in 1689 enact statute and ordaine "that no person nor persones within the Old Towne of Aberdeen or Chanonrie wasch any cloathes or anything els at any pairt of the Chanonrie from the head to the fute thereof, bot onlie at the backsyde, nixt the loch and that they sett ther fyres and wasching vessels ther, and throw out ther foull water on the South syde of the entrie of the said channel . . . as lykwyse that no persone wasch at any pairt of the Powies Burne . . . and siclyke dischairges all persones to Tramp and wash in tubs upon any pairt of the High street from the on [*sic*] end of the towne to the other and that under the penaltie of fourtie shilling Scot to be payit to the Thesr. for the use of the towne, and tuell shilling Scots to the officiars who are heirby impowered to poynd ther cloathes and wasching tubs thairfor whill they be payit and that for each transgressione toties quoties."

As we have seen, the Bishops of St. Machar's Cathedral were the Superiors of the City of Old Aberdeen, and as such nominated the Provost, Baillies, Sergeants, etc. The Council meetings were held in the Consistory House, which seems to have served as the Song School as well. The minutes give us a clear idea of a life very different from the life of to-day.

Apparently Old Aberdeen had been a walled city, as we find an Order in 1603, " Every indweller in this towne sall bigge upe the bak dykis for outhaulding of strangiers," and very severe punishment is threatened to anyone giving shelter to a stranger during the years of plague, 1604-1606.

The beer brewed in the Old Town was of a very fine quality, and many laws were passed by the Council as to the hours of selling. No drink is to be sold after 9 p.m., and none is to be sold at any time to the children attending the school. In 1605 a law was passed which might well be applied to the youth of to-day—" Na yeoung man within this towne that hes not ane hous or rent of his awn sall play at cartis, tabills, or dyss " upon penalty of forty shillings, or else sit upon the stool of repentance !

One of the town's officials was the " Scourger," an individual who may fairly be said to have earned his pay of 8/- a week. He is charged with the duty of keeping the town free of beggars — which must have been a very difficult job if we may judge from the number of edicts regarding them in the Town Council minutes. Probably the question of unemployment was, in a smaller way, quite as acute in the days of our forefathers as it is to-day; but in the 17th century there was no dole—it was " work " or " clear out." Yet the Town Council was not hard-hearted, for they drew a distinction between the able-bodied poor and those who were unable to work. To the latter was granted permission not only to remain in the town but " they shall come preceiselie and get almes at the yetis of honest men on such dayes allanerlie as they have or shall appoint for dealing thair almes and shall not molest thair yetis nor housses upon uther dayes under the pain of chastisment and removall aff of the towne." These privileged poor were known by the "townes marke on thair breastes, to wit ane floure de luce in leid."

The poor of the parish had a privilege granted to them also, which reads strangely in our ears, "They sall have thair awin marke viz., ane star in leid and sall have libertie to cum into the towne allanerlie on Sunday to heir the preiching and with this provisioun that thai come in to the kirke befoir the reading of the text and byd thair the time of the sermon, and if they be found on any weeke dayes in the towne in that caice to be punished as stranger beggars and chased away by the Scourger." Evidently the beggars were apt to be contumelious at times and to refuse to be chased away, in which case the Scourger "sall requyre two of the nearest neighbours to that place quhair the sturdy beggar is found to assist him, and in caice they refuis ther helps . . . they are ordainit to pay for thair penaltie thrie weekes wages toties quoties."

Scourging through the town was a fairly common punishment, but one which, so far as I can discover, was reserved for women. In almost all instances cases of theft are punished in this manner, and the victim is scourged through the whole town between the church and the Spital and then banished. Should she ever reappear she will be "brunit without doome or law." Some of the thefts seem to us hardly worthy of such a dire sentence; for instance, we have in 1671 the case of Christian Sutherland, a married woman, who pleads guilty to stealing " ane hank of fingering yarn from John Ross, Sacrist, King's College, as also ane long fisch and four cutts of salmon, all upon the fifth day of June." One wonders what had driven this poor woman to such an orgy of wickedness, all on a summer's day. Her punishment, which followed her sentence two days later, was " at two o'clock in the afternoon to be scourged through the town, banished, and never to be sene again ther upon pain of instant burning." The " good old days " left something to be desired.

We are told that " skolding and trubling of the towne be flyting is ane commond cours in Old Aberdeen," and it is decided that the guilty party shall pay a fine and " sall remain ane hour in the Gogis at the Cross." As the Scourger acted as Hangman too, we must allow that his job was no sinecure.

The domestic question raised its head even then. How true, O Solomon, there is nothing new under the sun. In 1643 we find the terms of an apprenticeship between William Dunn and Jean Mukart, his spous, on the one hand, and Elspet Gilcryst on the other. It is to last for seven years, and Elspet is to be provided " in mait, claith and intertenement," and is to be " learnt to waif schanks " in return for her work. Apparently clothing was part of the regular wages, for another entry tells us of Margaret Ellis receiving for her half-year's fee " four merks of silver withe cot and sleives, ane pair of schone, and ane new sark." Servants not quite content would seem to have had a trick of leaving their places without due notice, as the Town Council issues an order that every man or woman servant shall, six weeks before Whitsunday and Martinmas, "give lawful and timous advertisement to thir maisters or maistresses" whether they intend to stay for another six months. This is evidently the origin of a custom, now practically dead, known as Speaking Day, which was universal six weeks before the term not so very long ago.

CHAPTER IV.

THE University has played such an important part in the history of the town that a whole chapter must be devoted to it. I should like, however, here to draw the attention of my readers to the fact that the University was founded by Bishop Elphinstone, the most famous of the Cathedral Bishops, and, indeed, the foremost man of his time in Scotland. Bishop Elphinstone constituted himself and his successors in office Chancellors of the University. The Cathedral thus was head, not only of religious and secular affairs but of educational also. We shall see as we go on how the Church gradually lost this supreme power after the Reformation, but in Old Aberdeen at least there was always a very real spirit of concord between the Church, the Town Council and the University.

The upbringing and education of the children were matters of great concern to the Town Council, for till the days of the School Board, the schools were under the direct supervision of the ministers and kirk sessions throughout the country. Doubtless the youth of that day got into mischief just as it does to-day. In 1606 the " haill Infantorie within this towne sick as Arthure alias Wee Auld Thomas Robertson . . . sall compeer befoir the pulpit and sit down on thair knies, ask first God the congregation and thair fatheirs forgievance and sycklik it is statuit and ordained that the fathers of the said Infanterie sall within ilk fyfteen dayis delait thair bairnes liffis and behaweor to the bailzes."

We have no record of what the heinous sin of the poor, little Infanterie consisted to bring down upon them such dire punishment. To have to give an account to the baillies every fortnight of the doings of their children must have been a sore trial to the fathers.

It was evidently time to see about a new school-house, and the Council, which helped to pay the rent of the master, now resolved to give as much help as it could towards a new building. It was decided to build a new school of two storeys, the lower to be the ward-house or prison, the upper to be the Town Council room and school. The necessity for some sort of wardhouse is very apparent, as there was no prison for incarcerating persons guilty "of whatsumever crimes, whether thieving, scolding, cursing, swearing, Sabbath-breaking or the lyke" except "the Church," and it was felt by the Session that the house appointed for public worship and the service of God should no longer be "a receptacle for such persones."

The fee for being taught to read was fixed by the Provost and Baillies at 3/4. The Song School was regularly visited by them; the appointment of the master, who was also clerk, was made by the Session. In spite of the very small salary paid to the master, education must have been considered a paying profession, as several private schools were started, to the damage of the public school. The Provost and Baillies, taking this into their consideration, forbade parents to send their children to any but the public Musick School.

Some of the masters sought to eke out their income by various means, one even keeping the Public Change House. This did not commend itself to the Fathers of the town, who decreed that in future no master of the school shall keep "een common Change." Baillie William Baxter dissented.

The Grammar School, however, must have been quite a flourishing institution by the end of the 17th century. It can be seen in Slezer's Picture, a small building in front of King's College. In 1675 its fees were fixed at twelve shillings Scots to the master and the same sum to the doctor, quarterly, for each child. The value of money was so different in those days that it is difficult to realise what that would mean to-day, but it is interesting to see that the Grammar School had two teachers, one of whom is dignified by the title of Doctor.

The Council found it impossible to stop altogether the private schools, so they compromised—how truly British!—to the extent of allowing the Catechism and the Book of Proverbs to be taught in them, but nothing more. It is quite possible that some parents objected to the very long hours in vogue at the public school, which were 6-9, 10-12, and 2-6! The school was regularly inspected by members of the Kirk Session, Town Council and University. The particular needs of the girls were not looked after till 1723, although, doubtless, they attended the public school along with their brothers. At this date, however, a

Slezer's Old Aberdeen, 1683.

school was opened especially for them, in order that they might learn the science and art of sewing and needlework. The Town Council agreed to pay twenty pounds Scots, to enable the mistress to live.

It was represented to the University in 1738 that " the want of an accomplished gentlewoman for teaching white and coloured seam was an occasion of several gentlemen's sons being kept from this College, their parents inclining to send them where they might have suitable education for their daughters also." The University judged it reasonable to advance twelve pounds Scots to a Mrs. Cuthbert " residing in this town who had given sufficient proof of her capacity and diligence."

Some time in the 18th century the original Grammar School disappeared, and was succeeded by the building in School Road, known to many generations of boys as " The Barn." It consisted of one room, to which wings on either side were added later. In that one room about forty boys, from twelve years old and upwards, received their education. Most of the pupils remained for about five years, but many lads of more mature age came for only six months or so, before the Bursary Competition in November. Some of these pupils were bearded men, who had spent their lives on farms, studying in every spare moment and laying by every penny they could spare in the hope of some day " winnin' to the College." Can we wonder that the Barn turned out magnificent results, with such material to work on? The old Grammar School had, at various times, as Rectors men whose names were household words in the North of Scotland. The most famous of these are Ewen Maclachlan, who was also Librarian to the University, Mr. Fyfe and Dr. Dey.

The Gymnasium in the Chanonry was a boarding school as well as a day school. It attracted boys from the surrounding district as boarders, and many day boys came from Old and New Aberdeen. The rivalry between the two schools, the Gymnasium and the Grammar, found vent in many pitched battles, especially when snow lay thick on the ground. The Gym. boys were generally outclassed in the Bursary Competition by their rivals from the Barn, but it was their proud boast that the class prize lists reversed this priority. From both schools many lads who have played their part right nobly went forth into the world.

The Old Town shared in an endowment of Dr. Bell, Chaplain in the East India Service, by means of which a school for boys and girls was carried on from 1832 till the educational system of the country was put under the charge of the School Board. Old Aberdeen now possesses a very fine Primary School, where excellent work is done by a large staff of teachers. Cookery, laundrywork and needlework are part of the curriculum for the girls, while the boys are taught carpentry.

When one considers that the children of the professors and ministers required to be educated, that there was no means of communication between the two towns, and that families *were* families in those happy days—a round dozen being no uncommon thing—one realises that for the children of the professional class something had to be done in Old Aberdeen for their primary education. At one time the need was met by one of the masters of the Gymnasium giving up an hour or two every morning to the younger children, whose big brothers attended the school. Very happy mornings these were for the children; I fear that for the unfortunate master they must have been something of a nightmare. To drive the elements of reading, writing, geography and arithmetic into the heads of about twenty small boys and girls, aged from five to nine years, in one room, and that not a large one, was too much to ask of any unfortunate master. I should think Mr. Thomson must have been very glad when a call to a parish relieved him from his class of Old Town children. A school was then opened by two ladies, daughters of a farmer in Dyce, well-educated, highly refined gentlewomen. Their school did splendid work for nearly half a century. Their interest in the children who passed through their hands was very keen, and to the last day of their lives the Misses Bowman could tell you whose birthday it was, and in what quarter of the globe each scattered member of their flock could be found. It was through no weakness of theirs that the school had to be given up; the work done by the Misses Bowman and the high ideal of honour and duty they set before their pupils cannot be too highly praised. Their school was run on old-fashioned lines; they had little sympathy with Montessori and P.N.E.U. systems. They taught the children, however, that there is no royal road to learning, and that the harder the lesson the more honour there was in mastering it. Tramways and 'buses have made communication so easy that now there is no possibility of a school succeeding in Old Aberdeen; indeed, we may say that the days of private teachers are a thing of the past.

CHAPTER V.

WE must now retrace our steps to the very troublous times which came upon our country in the 17th and 18th centuries. The history of the towns of Old and New Aberdeen is indeed very much the history of Scotland from the time of Queen Mary right on to the beginning of the 19th century, when the dread of a French invasion and the preparations for repelling it kept all the coast towns in a state of armed defence. "Ther wes no citie in Scotland which did suffer more hurt than Aberdeen did, nor oftener" in the Civil Wars which shook the country from end to end after the Reformation. The Covenanting struggles were particularly felt in Aberdeen where so many, including the famous "Aberdeen Doctors," refused to sign the Covenant, insisting upon freedom of conscience for everyone. Nine separate times was Aberdeen taken and retaken; the wonder is, not that it did not grow during those centuries but that it was able to survive at all. In all these struggles Old Aberdeen had to bear its share, and its troubles were greatly increased by there being no governing body at its head to look after the interests of the community. We have seen that the Bishop of the Cathedral was also the head of the town; on him fell the duty of choosing suitable men to look after its interests. After the foundation of King's College and University, of which also the Bishop was the head, he could count upon the support of the regents and doctors, so that we need not be surprised when we find in later and more peaceful days that the Town Council of Old Aberdeen was never without at least one professor or principal, either as provost, baillie or councillor. In these bad times, however, of which we are speaking, the town was left without a Council or any means of summoning one. When the Roman Catholic Bishop was succeeded by an Episcopal Bishop, he inherited the duty of looking after the town in things secular as well as spiritual, but the clash of conflicting opinions between the Crown, the Church and the people left long intervals when the Bishop was unable to do anything for his flock. It is impossible for me to give any account of the Civil Wars which raged in our country during the 17th and 18th centuries. Every student of history must be conversant with them, although it is extremely difficult to follow all the intrigues, plots and factions of these troubled times. The Town Council minutes are very brief and scanty, and the fact that two volumes are missing—that from 1617-1634 and that from 1728-1738—makes it more difficult for us to construct the history of our town.

We know that in 1639 Bishop Bellenden had to flee the city, taking with him as much of his furniture and plate as he could carry away. At this time, too, it was considered safer to close the University; Principal, professors and students all scattered.

In 1644 Old Aberdeen was taxed for the outfitting of twelve foot soldiers and one horseman who were to march with Captain M'Nab into England against the

English. "Ilk soldier was furnished with two sarks, coat and breeks, hose and bonnet, bands and shoon, a sword and musket, powder and ball for so many, and others some a sword and pike, and ilk soldier to have six shillings every day for the space of forty days of loan silver." An armed trooper with his horse cost one hundred and eighty-six pounds thirteen and four-pence. Spalding remarks, "Sore was the poor people of the Old Town plucked and poinded to make up these soldiers' charges, whereas some of them had not to [*sic*] buy a loaf." Neither herd nor hire-man was left untaxed; a troop of horsemen was quartered in the town till the money was all paid. We are told that the Baillies had to advance this money out of their own pockets to get rid of the guard. The danger was, however, so pressing that the Council thought it necessary to provide a drill-master at twenty-four shillings a day "to learn the poor bodies to handle their arms, who had more need to handle the plough." An inventory of the town's arms shows "nine firelock guns, ten halberts, two swords and two banderts with two militia muskets, two picks and other two swords, all burnt with the town's Arms."

The 13th of September, 1644, was a day that brought sorrow and doull to both the towns of Aberdeen. On the 12th Montrose with his army marched down Deeside and encamped at Two-Mile Cross. In the morning he demanded peaceable entrance, in order to read His Majesty's Proclamation. A meeting was summoned by the Provost, when an answer was prepared. Montrose's messengers were, according to

Spalding, "causit to drink hardlie, and be the way the drummer was unhappelie slayne." Montrose, "heighlie offendit," fell upon the town. He defeated its army between the Crabstane and the Justice Mylnes and delivered it to his Irish soldiers, who burned and plundered for four days. These soldiers wore in their caps "ane rip of oates." Spalding says, "Oure towne's people began to weir the lyke in ther bonnetis and to knyt to till the knokis of oure yettis the lyke rip of oates; bot it was littill saifgaird to us." He also tells us that he "saw tua corpis careit to the buriall throw the Old Town with wemen onlie, and not ane man amongst them." The outcome of this terrible defeat had been presaged the night before "the moone ross alls reid as blood tuo houris befoir hir tyme." The end of the trouble was not yet, for a very few days later the Duke of Argyll arrived with his army "quhairof thair wes quarterit on poor Old Abirdeen Argile's own thrie regiments." Spalding goes on to tell us that the first night the officers and gentlemen drank up all the ale and "levit upone wort thairefter." The General Assembly of the Church, meeting in Edinburgh in January, 1648, ordered a fast to be held on the first Sunday of the year, that prayer might be offered to Almighty God for the unhappy state of the country. Spalding says that the second Sunday was also ordered to be held as a fast in Old Aberdeen, whereby "the poor people were vexed to death with their continual fastings and thanksgivings."

In 1669 we have the first mention of the Militia. Old Aberdeen provided four men to the Aberdeen Company, called together in consequence of the war with Holland to protect the port and town. These militia-men must, to a certain extent at least, have been supplied by the local lairds. Mrs. Helen Cullen, owner of some land near the Don, being a widow was called upon to supply a fifth man. Very soon afterwards she petitioned that "as she is now clothed with a husband" the militiaman is unnecessary. Her petition was granted.

Showing the very unsettled state of affairs that all these civil wars had brought about, we find that in 1688 it was necessary to have an armed guard, watching over the town by night, and to have all men capable of bearing arms instructed in their use. A daily rendezvous of twenty-four of the Old Town's men was called to meet at the bowling green of King's College at three o'clock of the afternoon in order that they might be drilled. In 1782 Lord Shelborne promulgated a plan for arming the principal towns of Scotland. This plan was agreed to by the Town Council, who called for volunteers. A military association was formed, a constitution was framed, and officers were appointed. Major Mitchell, formerly an officer in His Majesty's service, was chosen to be Commandant, Captain Gray to be Captain, Hugh Leslie of Powis to be Lieutenant, and Mr. Volum, Convener of Trades, to be Ensign. Seventy volunteers at once joined, a large proportion, as it was estimated that the whole number of able-bodied men was only one hundred and seventy.

Apparently this military association did not last very long, for in 1798, when the dread of a French invasion was at its height, we find that the Provost and Town Council, "having taken under their serious consideration the present danger of the country from the threatened invasion of the French, our inveterate enemy," resolved to recommend to the inhabitants to prepare themselves for rendering personal services in defence of the King and country in the most efficacious manner. The Council recorded their thanks to Provost Leslie for his suggestion of these resolutions and resolved also that they should be published in the "Aberdeen Journal."

A corps of Old Aberdeen Volunteers was formed. The "London Gazette" contained the following announcement:—"Commissions in the Old Aberdeen Volunteer Association—Alexander Matheson, Captain; Gilbert Gerard, First Lieutenant; Dr. William Jack, Second." Although Alexander Matheson, one of the Magistrates, was nominally the Captain of the Company, the real Commander was Dr. Gilbert Gerard. He was Professor first of Greek and then of Divinity in King's College, and was one of the ministers of St. Machar's Cathedral. He graduated at King's College in 1777, and came back to the Old Town as Professor in 1790, and in 1791 was enrolled as a Burgess. If one may judge of the man from his portrait, one must feel that only a very strong sense of duty and of the necessity for such service would have made Professor Gilbert Gerard accept a commission in a Volunteer Regiment, yet he commanded the Old Aberdeen Volunteers from 1798 till the Company was disbanded in 1802. His accoutrements may be seen in the Museum of Marischal College; the banner of the Company, worked by his daughters, is preserved in King's College Chapel. An excellent account of the Gerard family, written by the late Mrs. Harrower, will be found in the Aberdeen University Review, Vol. X.

It is a truism that history repeats itself, but it is interesting to recall here that the Rev. Bruce M'Ewen, Ph.D., Second Minister of the Cathedral in 1914, was also a Captain in a Territorial Regiment, that as such he joined up with his men at the outbreak of the Great War, and served all through the years of the War. He found it necessary to resign his ministerial charge when he felt in 1916 that the War was not likely to come to an end very soon. After the Armistice he received a unanimous call from the congregation of the Cathedral to the First Charge, made vacant by the resignation of the Rev. Dr. Calder. The strain of the War, alas, proved too much for his strength, and he passed away in 1923—

"Sed miles sed pro Patria."

No such hardships had to be endured by the Old Aberdeen Volunteer Company, under Captain Gerard. The first appearance of this Corps was in 1798 on the occasion of Nelson's victory at the Battle of the Nile, when they marched in front of the Town House and fired three volleys, which, although it was their first attempt at firing, they performed with exactness! They returned in the evening, and after having fired three more volleys they were entertained by the Provost and Magistrates of the city.

In 1800 they were inspected by the Duke of Gordon and received their Colours from Major-General Hay. In 1802 they decided to join the Aberdeen Volunteers, of whose history a most interesting account is given by the late Donald Sinclair.

CHAPTER VI.

One of the duties which had to be undertaken by the Town Council and its officials in those days, when there were no steam hooters and whistles making morning hideous, was to arouse the sleepers from their beds and get them started to their work. Early hours were evidently the order of the day, if one may judge from the time when the children went to school and the students to their studies, so that some sort of wakening was very necessary. Up to the middle of the 17th century this was accomplished by a bell-ringer, who went through the town at 5 a.m. to rouse the people for their daily work, and again at 9 p.m., when, the day's duties done, it was evidently considered that all good town's folk should be at home and in bed. In 1662, however, the Treasurer was ordered to buy a suit of clothes with a pair of shoes for the Drummer, to whom evidently this duty had been handed. He must have looked very fine indeed, as his suit consisted of "ane long coat of ane purple collour with quhyt lace therupon with breiches and stockings of that same collour, and ane pair double solled shoes." One would have thought he would have been only too glad to show off these beautiful clothes, but perhaps familiarity bred contempt for, in 1687, there were many complaints against him for not doing his duty. The Baillies therefore enacted that if he should anyways fail in doing his duty by not going through the town and beating the drum "ilk morning and evening at the ordinar times and seasons, useit and wont, the weather being dry and he in health"! that twelve pennies of his salary shall be retained every day by the Trades. In 1830 it was decided to use a bugle instead of a drum, but that cannot have been found so satisfactory, for one of my earliest recollections is of watching the drummer marching up the High Street, attracting the attention of the citizens by his shouts of "Oyez, Oyez, Oyez," and then announcing that something had been lost or found.

I have referred to the difficulty in which the town was placed when it had no governing body. In 1690 the Magistrates and Town Council appealed to the Privy Council, asking that they might be confirmed in their places and given authority to watch over the affairs of the town. Their petition was granted, and the privilege was conferred in 1719 by King George I., and again in 1729 by George II., in a Charter, giving, granting and committing to them the usual and necessary powers within the said Borough . . . With power to them by a majority of voices yearly to elect their own successors "aye and while We, our Heirs and Successors see fit to revoke the forsaid power or give any other direction in the said matter."

Being thus confirmed in their positions the Provost and Town Council looked after the interests of Old Aberdeen for almost two hundred years, when an Act of Parliament decreed that Old Aberdeen must cease to exist as a separate community. But more of this hereafter. Meantime we are concerned with the manner in which the Provost and Baillies carried out their duties. In 1728 there was a vacancy in one of the Cathedral charges, when the Kirk Session appealed to the Town Council to join with them and the masters of the College in a deputation to the Presbytery, to ask for a free choice in the election of a minister. The Town Council agreed and appointed some of its members to join the deputation. It was right enough that the Town Council should have a voice in the choice of a minister, as they sat in the Cathedral in a loft or gallery of their own. Not only that, but on the occasion of a new Provost taking his seat, it was the custom for them to march up to the Cathedral from the Town House, for the "Kirking of the Council." As the professors also attended divine worship in the Cathedral it was much to their interest also to have a suitable minister.

I have already alluded to the water difficulty, which became fairly acute in the 18th century. The water springs to the west of Old Aberdeen were acquired from the University, but it was felt that a reservoir for the water was absolutely necessary. The Town Council, after visiting the ground floor of the prison, agreed that it was not only the most commodious place for the purpose but that its use would save "a deal of expense to the town." The plan was approved, and it was resolved that the prison be upon the third storey, the second storey being used for meetings of the Town Council and Trades. Apparently the plan was not so economical as our good Fathers had hoped, for by the end of the 18th century they accepted an estimate of three hundred and thirty pounds to rebuild the Town House.

There was evidently great need for economy at this time. The Council decided that, considering the small funds of the town, they were unable to pay the entertainments usually given on certain occasions, especially on the nights of the two markets. It was decided, therefore, to pay four pounds Scots to the men that mounted guard, which could be used by them as they thought proper.

In 1796 the Provost informed the Council that a roll of inhabitants had been taken which showed that there were eleven hundred persons in Old Aberdeen, and that the value of their rents was five hundred and forty pounds fifteen shillings. The Provost went on to point out that many complaints had been received as to the badness of the streets and lanes of the city, and that the only money available was required for the lighting of the streets in winter. He said it was very desirable to have the streets properly causewayed, that they ought to have a foot pavement, and better lighting. He therefore suggested that the inhabitants should assess themselves for twenty-one years at the rate of one shilling per pound of their rents, in order to pave and light the streets and supply the city with water. He also suggested that trustees be appointed by those who contributed to carry out the scheme. This proposal was unanimously agreed to, and a vote of thanks was passed to the Provost, Hugh Leslie of Powis, for the amount of trouble he had taken in this affair.

The proposed union of King's and Marischal Colleges caused our Town Council much anxiety. The first hint of this suggestion reached them in 1786, when they "fully and maturely considered the plan," and came unanimously to the opinion that it would not be productive of the advantages "it set furth," but, "on the contrary, will be hurtful to the country and prejudicial to the interests of education"; and seeing that this scheme cannot be brought about without the subversion of the chartered rights of a venerable University which has subsisted in our city for near three centuries with honour and reputation, "We, the Provost, Magistrates and Council, must express our disapprobation," etc., etc. They resolved to send a copy of the present "Act" to the Right Hon. Lord Sydney, Secretary of State, and further they decided "to make every legal and constitutional opposition to so unpreceedented and ruinous a measure."

The scheme is not mentioned again in the Town Council minutes for nearly a hundred years. In 1854 the Town Council addressed a Memorial to the Earl of Aberdeen, Prime Minister, pointing out how closely they have watched the measures that have been taken for effecting a union between King's College and Marischal College. In this Memorial they point out that they regard the University and College as the chief ornaments of their city, and the sources of its prosperity; they look with jealousy on any interference with the privileges which, through a succession of ages, have been transmitted to them. They are quite sensible of the anomalous position which the two Colleges hold among the Universities of Scotland; they point out the advantages of New Aberdeen for the study of Law and Medicine and the advantages of Old Aberdeen for the Faculty of Arts. They conclude by expressing their entire confidence in Lord Aberdeen's knowledge of the subject and in the integrity and sincerity which have distinguished his whole life as a Peer of Parliament and as a Minister of State.

The union of the Universities was carried through in 1858, very much in the manner suggested by Old Aberdeen. For many years the appearance of the Old Town was not changed by the union. Want of accommodation, however, led to the necessity of new buildings. New King's was erected on the site of the Aulton Brewery, which brewed such famous ale. An old friend living in the High Street lamented its parting sorely in these words, "We would hae been better wantin' the University than wantin' the brewery"! So much for the privilege of living in a University town.

Further extensions are being carried on meantime, owing to the very rapid increase in the number of students since the union, and since the admission of women to the privileges of University training. A beautiful new hall for examination and other purposes is rapidly nearing completion.

The union of the Universities preluded a union which meant even more to the little community of Old Aberdeen. For long the Town Council had been faced with the great difficulty — indeed, one may say the impossibility—of raising sufficient funds for lighting, policing, and bringing water to the town. The higher standard of living required that water be brought to the houses, and the suggestion that bathrooms were a necessity was even being hinted. The supply of water was very much limited owing to the purchase by the Great North of Scotland Railway of the ground where the springs were situated. People demanded that the street lamps be lighted every night in winter, whereas the Town Council had funds to do so only when no moon was expected!

The charitable funds in which Old Aberdeen has always been wealthy attracted from the poorer parts of Aberdeen some of the less desirable inhabitants, and it was found that the half policeman, which was all the Town Council could afford, was not sufficient. To add to these difficulties, democracy began to raise its head even in conservative Old Aberdeen, and there was a demand from some of the more advanced young men that they should have a choice in the election of the Town Council, thus striking at the very roots of our ancient constitution. Under the circumstances the Town Council thought it better to call a public meeting and lay the whole matter before the people. The impossibility of imposing higher taxes or of improving the public services as things stood was pointed out, while the advantages of union, better paved roads, better lighting, and a better water supply were demonstrated. It was decided to take a plebiscite of the inhabitants, with the result that 100 voted for amalgamation, 126 against, while 42 did not answer at all. In 1887, however, Old Aberdeen agreed to amalgamation under certain conditions, and in 1891, under an Act of Parliament incorporating it with Aberdeen, it ceased to have an independent existence.

In appearance Old Aberdeen has not changed much, although of late years many houses have been built in the immediate vicinity. High Street, Chanonry, and Don Street remain much as they have done for long. The Cathedral Towers and King's College Crown are still our distinctive feature, while the much more modern Powis towers and gateway give a very quaint touch to College Bounds. Powis towers give rise to much speculation, and no one can say what was the idea in the mind of their designer. Some attribute their curious architecture to the rage for Byron and all things Eastern at the beginning of the 19th century, when they were built. The crescent on the top is the family crest of the Frasers from whom the Leslies of Powis were descended. The quaint, old Hermitage upon its hill, so long a feature of Old Aberdeen, is now, alas! no more, and with it have passed away the many legends, more or less fanciful, which tried to account for it.

I cannot conclude this chapter on Old Aberdeen better than by quoting the following poem by Dr. Arthur Johnston, 1685:—

THE OLD TOWN.

(Vulgarly) called Old Aberdeen.

A pious Bishop lives and rules in thee.
Don makes thee prosperous,
And the neighbouring sea.

Don by a wondrous bridge is overlaid,
Of one arch, which the Gods belike have made.
Such was the Rhodian Coloss work of old,
Where ships with hoised sails to pass were bold :
Near this the salmon swim, and snares are set
For them, and they are catcht in every net.
In thee an old and stately temple stands,
The rest demolisht are by strangers' hands :
That temple with two towers doth rise, which be
(as Pharos guids) to travellers at Sea :
Phoebus and Pallas Palaces not far,
From that fair Temple to be viewed are.
Buildings fit for these guests and over them
There is a guilded cross and diadem.
An Holy Bishop raised this Fabrick, which
The King did with fair revenues enrich.
And Rome which doth by words her bounty show
Did names of Honour upon them bestow.
So many Greeks (who ruined Troy by force)
Did not brake forth out of the Trojan horse :
As that brave house of Learning hath brought forth,
Of Shining lights, and men of greatest Worth.
Thou dost not need thy Praises should be sung
Thou Noble Town by any Stranger's tongue;
Since by this people who reside in thee,
Thine Honour fitly published can be.

ST. MACHAR'S CATHEDRAL

It must be quite evident to anyone who has read the foregoing pages on Old Aberdeen that the town owed its very existence to the Cathedral Church of St. Machar. I have already alluded to the legend which caused St. Machar to settle here and build the first little church.

Nectanus, who had been Bishop in Mortlach for some fourteen years, was the first Bishop of the Cathedral, but what sort of a church he came to we have no idea. Boethius tells us that St. Machar built a chapel where the present Cathedral now stands. Neither Nectanus nor his two immediate successors did anything towards building a new church. It was not till 1163 that Bishop Matthew Kininmonth began to build a church which he hoped would be more worthy of its position, and which he intended to dedicate to the memory of St. Machar. This Bishop Matthew Kininmonth had been the Archdeacon of the Cathedral in St. Andrews. To him Malcolm IV. granted a Charter giving to the Cathedral Church "the haill vill of Old Aberdeen with the kirk of Kirkton and the pertinents," also many other kirks in the neighbourhood, also the tithe of the King's "own revenues and all the escheats belonging to me betwixt the two waters called Dee and Spey." This Charter was confirmed by

William the Lion, who added to it " the land of Brass, now called Birse, with the forest thereof."

Matthew Kininmonth's Church was pulled down by Bishop Henry Cheyne on the ground that it was not " glorious enough." He began another church which shared the same fate at the hands of his successor, Bishop Alexander Kininmonth, 1357-1381. This Bishop Alexander Kininmonth was the second of the name. The first Alexander Kininmonth succeeded Bishop Cheyne in 1327. He built two Episcopal palaces, one to the east of the Cathedral and another at Fetternear. The latter was probably for use as a summer residence and also to allow the Bishop to make closer acquaintance with the large district over which he presided. The palace in the Cathedral grounds was burned in 1333, when the English soldiers set fire to Aberdeen, which burned for six days. In 1357 Alexander Kininmonth the Second was created Bishop of the Cathedral. His first step was to pull down part of the edifice and to begin a building on a larger scale than had been contemplated before. To raise funds for this purpose the Dean and Chapter had been collecting for some years, and had themselves contributed sixty pounds a year from their stipends. It is interesting to note that Barbour, author of " The Bruce," was one of the Chapter at the time. The Pope made a liberal grant of indulgences, and King Robert the Bruce himself, who never forgot what he owed to his loyal subjects in Aberdeen, gave as much help as he could. But in spite of all these efforts the money collected was sufficient only to raise the walls of the nave a few feet above the ground, when Alexander Kininmonth died. The work seems to have been at a standstill till 1424, when Henry Leighton, Bishop of Moray, was appointed to the See. He completed the walls of the nave, built St. John's Chapel in the north transept—in which 17 years later he was buried—and built the twin towers. The good work was carried on by his successor, Bishop Lindsay, who paved the church with freestone and roofed it with red fir. Bishop Spens, who was translated from Galloway, was the keeper of the Privy Seal. We are told that he was a man of "an active spirit." His first step was to repair the Bishop's palace, but he was far from unmindful of the church. He erected stalls in the chancel, along with a beautiful chair for the Bishop's use, and he put glass in the windows which must have been an enormous boon to the congregation!

Bishop Spens was succeeded by Bishop Elphinstone, the most famous of all our Bishops. He built the great central tower, of which, alas, we have no picture, and he covered the roof with lead. Orem tells us that the great tower whose foundations had been laid by Bishop Leighton fifty-nine years before "was built four-square and four storey high. It contained a little four-cornered chamber, above which was a square tower with a stang on the top of it, five ells in length, with a great globe of brass above the first cross of the said stang; and above the second cross was a cock, an ell in length, of brass and his breast of copper, which stang, globe and cock Mr. David Corse, a Presbyterian minister of this church, disposed of."

As Orem wrote about 1725 and the great tower stood till 1688, there is every reason to believe his account. In the tower Elphinstone hung three great bells and many smaller ones, and to his efforts we owe the fact that the whole roof was covered with lead, which proved a great temptation later. Elphinstone now turned his attention to the condition of the choir, which Robert the Bruce is reported to have condemned as unworthy of so great a Cathedral. The Bishop died, however, before he had finished his work, broken-hearted by the misery brought upon Scotland by the fatal field of Flodden. His clergy, inspired by his example, finished the choir and built the high altar. Bishop Gavin Dunbar, 1519-1532, built the south transept, which was called his aisle. He added spires to Bishop Leighton's twin towers, and he ceiled the church with "the finest oak, of such excellent work that there is scarce any like it to be seen in this Kingdom." Tradition says that this wonderful roof cost eight pounds, Scots money, a large sum in those days. For a full account of the Cathedral roof I must refer my readers to the description given by Principal Sir William Geddes in the volume of the New Spalding Club called "The Heraldic Ceiling of the Cathedral."

The roof is adorned with forty-eight shields, arranged in three rows. The centre row shows the shields of His Holiness Pope Leo X., the thirteen Bishops of Scotland, the Prior of St. Andrews, and the Arms of the University. To the right are the shields of Charles, Emperor of the Holy Roman Empire, thirteen Sovereigns of Europe, the Duke of Bourbon, and the Arms of Old Aberdeen. On the left we have the shield of James V., Queen Margaret, the Scottish Nobles, and the Arms of Aberdeen. On the border below the roof are painted—on the north side a succession of the Bishops of Aberdeen from Nectanus to William Gordon, the last Catholic Bishop, 1577; on the south side the names of the Sovereigns from Malcolm II. to Queen Mary.

Bishop Dunbar's tomb still remains, and is the most beautiful in workmanship of all the monuments in the Cathedral.

To Bishop Stewart, his successor, we owe the Consistory House in the Cathedral. He left his name on the walls. Orem says that it was "lately obliterated by the plastering and washing of the walls of the church"; and the same writer tells us that from the Consistory House "there is an entry to a secret room under the North lesser steeple, called the Charter House." The beautifully carved pulpit given by Bishop Stewart to the Cathedral may now be seen in the Chapel of King's College.

We have traced the story of the building of the church through the centuries, and we have seen that it owed everything to the care and generosity of those who loved it and all it stood for. Begun in 1357 it was not completed till 1530, and yet this glorious church which had taken so long to build, and which embodied so much faith, patience, and self-denial, remained in its full beauty for only twenty years. In 1530 it consisted of a nave, side aisles, north and south transepts, with the beginning of a choir or chancel. It seems very doubtful whether this was ever finished. The great central tower, 150 feet in height, and the twin towers made the Cathedral a very conspicuous landmark for ships at sea and for travellers approaching Aberdeen over the slopes of the Grampians.

Beautiful and great in itself, the Cathedral was very wealthy. It possessed a store of gold and silver chalices and crucifixes, set with precious stones; it also had many vestments embroidered with gold thread and decorated with jewels. Parson Gordon says that "the weight of all this was very great and hardly to be believed were it not that an old manuscript yet extant contains a full account of all that belonged to the Church."

The troubles which had been foreseen for Scotland by Bishop Elphinstone had been accumulating during the reign of James V. The principles of the Reformed Faith, adopted by England, were spreading in Scotland, whose people were growing weary of the wealth, idleness, and corruption of the clergy. The Scottish Bishops strove to bring about a rupture with England, as they dreaded the influence of Henry VIII. over James; he could not afford to quarrel with the Bishops who helped to keep the great nobles in check. The result of all this was the Battle of Solway Moss, where the Scots were absolutely defeated, and from which James crept to his palace at Falkland, where he died in 1542 at the early age of thirty-one, a few days after the birth of Mary Queen of Scots. The Scottish Parliament absolutely refused to ratify the promise of

Regent Arran that Mary should marry Prince Edward of England. War broke out once more, and the English invaded Scotland in 1544.

In order to save the ornaments and jewels belonging to the Cathedral, Bishop Stewart sent them with an escort of priests into the country across the Don. On the grassy slope above the bridge the priests were attacked by Forbes of Corsendae with an armed band, who forcibly seized the jewels and carried them off. It is strange now to think of such a struggle taking place at the peaceful Brig o' Balgownie. Forbes' idea had apparently been to hold the jewels for ransom, as he agreed to restore them to the Bishop on the payment of six hundred merks. Unfortunately, greed proved too strong for his honesty; he took the six hundred merks but restored only half of his ill-gotten gains. For this sacreligious act he was excommunicated, and "his family never prospered thereafter." As times grew yet more troublous, it was considered safer to entrust the remaining chalices and other silver plate to the charge of the Canons, while the Bishop's mitres, sacred vestments and gold and silver ornaments were handed over to the Earl of Huntly for safe keeping. The storm broke in 1560, when the Cathedral was invaded by a mob of the townspeople, led by the Barons of the Mearns, who, having plundered and destroyed the abbeys in New Aberdeen, marched over to Old Aberdeen and fell upon the Cathedral, which they stripped of any ornaments and jewels that had been left. They demolished the chancel, at the end of which stood the high altar; they stripped the lead off the roof and carried away the bells, the gift of Bishop Elphinstone, from the great tower. Laden with their booty, they set off for Holland, but, by the vengeance of Heaven, the ship had hardly left the harbour when she sank, and the whole crew was drowned off the Girdleness. The church would have been completely destroyed at this time had not the Earl of Huntly and Leslie of Balquhain appeared upon the scene with a large armed force and driven away the rioters. Fetternear, the Bishop's palace in the country, was given to Leslie as a reward for his timely assistance.

It took some years to repair the damage done to the Cathedral, but by 1607 it was put in good order again. The high altar was erected against the east wall of Bishop Dunbar's Aisle, as the chancel had been destroyed. The roof was covered with slates to replace the lead which had been stolen.

One of the most venerated possessions of the Cathedral was a statue of the Virgin Mary with the Babe, carved in wood. It hung above the high altar, and Bishop Chisholm has given us a most interesting account of it. He says that for more than six hundred years it had been an object of veneration to the faithful. Many miracles were wrought by it, and pilgrims came from far and near to implore the protection of "Our Lady of Aberdeen." When Bishop Dunbar completed the bridge over the Dee, for which Bishop Elphinstone had left a large sum of money, he built a little chapel on the first arch. In it he placed the statue which he had caused to be solemnly translated from the Cathedral to its new sanctuary. Not far from the chapel there sprang up a little fountain of limpid water with miraculous powers. One day, however, a heretic defiled the water, for which blasphemous deed he was instantly punished by Almighty God, but Bishop Dunbar, to protect the statue from the risk of such profanation, removed it once more to the Cathedral and placed it in the Lady Chapel in Dunbar's Aisle. The miraculous powers continued, for in 1520 it prophesied to Bishop Dunbar the calamities that were to befall Scotland. One hundred years after the death of the Bishop his tomb was opened; it was found then that his body had escaped dissolution and that he bore no sign of corruption. The statue of Our Lady escaped damage from the sacreligious hands of the mob who destroyed so much else in the Cathedral. For greater safety, however, it was hidden by some of the faithful sons of the church till it was possible to get it conveyed out of the country. About 1625 it was placed on a ship to be entrusted to the care of the Archduchess Isabella, Governess of the Low Countries. The ship was struck by a terrible tempest, which practically made a wreck of her, but by the mercy of Heaven she reached Dunkirk, although without either mast or sails. The miraculous powers conferred on Our Lady of Aberdeen manifested themselves even in a foreign country. Wonderful miracles were wrought, and crowds came to pay their devotion to "Our Lady of Succour, or Good Success," as she is sometimes called. The statue may be seen in the Church of Finnesterre in Brussels, in a side chapel. The inventory of the Cathedral specially mentions the dress of Our Lady and that of the Babe as being very fine and ornamented with jewels.

The Cathedral library, which would have been of such enormous interest to antiquarians, was destroyed about 1560—" All wes taken away or destroyed or embaseled; the bibliothec then burned and no book spared wher any reid letter was to be seene."

Before we pass on to the story of the Cathedral after the Reformation, let us try to visualise the life lived in and around the church in Roman Catholic days. We have seen that the Bishop had his palace a little to the east of the Cathedral, while his chaplain occupied one side of the chaplains' chambers, from which an underground passage led to the palace. Opposite the palace was the Chancellor's manse. It was used as a dwelling house till the end of the 19th century, when it was bought by Mr. Leslie of Fetternear, who, unmindful surely of what he owed to the Cathedral, pulled down this very interesting old house. The manses of the other prebends were very much smaller, and have entirely disappeared. There were originally twelve of these; the number was later increased to nineteen by Bishop Cheyne and Bishop Alexander Kininmonth.

Next in importance to the Bishop was the Dean; then came the Precentor, the Chancellor, the Treasurer, the Archdeacon, the minor Canons and the Sacrist. It was the duty of the Treasurer to keep the Cathedral plate and to provide all lights and candles. The Archdeacon had the charge of " the manners of the clergy," while the duties of the Sacrist were manifold. Bishop

St. Machar's Cathedral, showing Manses of
Chancellor and Prebend.

Elphinstone, who had found a good deal amiss in the Cathedral worship, insisted that the Sacrist should be a priest and should be present every day with the other vicars at service. It was his duty to see that the Cathedral bell was rung before 5 a.m. every morning, summer and winter, also to have the great bells rung on Feast Days. He was responsible also for the clock being kept up to time, for the vestments of the clergy and the books of the choir. He had also to keep "the windows of the church from all blots and the walls from all dust and mousewebs four times a year, . . . also the church that doves and ravens come not in . . . also to provide palms on Palm Sunday and to prevent the scholars carrying away the cups from the Choir after Holy Communion." For all these many duties he was paid twelve pounds a year so long as his services were satisfactory, but should he be negligent in the performance of his duty the fourth part of his yearly salary was to be subtracted by the Chapter.

The chaplains' court was built by Bishop Gavin Dunbar, whose armorial coat is still to be seen on the wall of the only remaining portion. The house was originally a four-sided building, and is said to have contained rooms for twenty or more chaplains, who all dined at a common table. A small tower or turret stood at each corner; the well was in the centre of the square. Orem tells us that at the Reformation the chaplains' chambers fell into the hands of a layman. Later Bishop Patrick Forbes of Corse used it as a divinity college; the divinity students as well as their professor lived in it and were taught there.

The mention of Bishop Forbes takes us to the Reformation, which brought such disastrous results to the Cathedral and to the Chanonry of Old Aberdeen. William Gordon, the last Roman Catholic Bishop, died in 1577. He was succeeded by the Episcopalian Bishops, of whom Bishop Forbes of Corse, 1618-1635, was the fourth. He was the most famous of the "Aberdeen Doctors," and according to Spottiswoode was "the best Prelate that Scotland had seen since Elphinstone." During his occupation of the Bishop's Chair, comparative peace seems to have settled upon the church, so that Bishop Forbes was able to give a good deal of attention to the affairs of King's College, of which he was Chancellor, in his capacity of Bishop of Aberdeen.

Bishop Forbes was succeeded by Bishop Bellenden, who was deposed and excommunicated by the Glasgow Assembly in 1638, along with the Bishops of Edinburgh, Glasgow, St. Andrews, and other places, much to the indignation of the King, who pointed out that the Assembly was itself without authority, as it was held without any bishops being present. The Church paid no attention to this, and ordered its findings to be read in all the parish churches, which was done except in "brave Aberdeen which would have none of them." Bishop Bellenden remained in his palace facing the storm till the spring of 1639, when, gathering together as much of his worldly goods as possible he fled to New Aberdeen! Shortly afterwards, however, he was obliged to leave the country. Showing the very unsettled state of the church at this time, it is interesting to notice that Dr. Scrogie, minister of the Cathedral, gave great offence by celebrating the Communion on Christmas Day, 1638, which had been forbidden by the Assembly, and that the son of Bishop Bellenden had to be buried " without ane funerall sermon."

In the bad years that followed, Old Aberdeen suffered terribly because of its dependence upon the Cathedral, which had been deprived of its Bishop in 1638. The next year King's College lost its Principal, Dr. Leslie, who was deposed because he would not sign the Covenant. Spalding tells us that in March, 1639, Dr. Leslie, along with some others, fled to England by sea, and that the sub-Principal and Regents " kest up the Colledge yettis, set the students at libertie and fled throw the countrie themselfis."

Following the example of the College, the Grammar Schools, Song Schools and other schools closed their doors, " and the Barnes were had hame to thair parentis. No lerning at all, feiring alteratiouns and trubles to cum, as cam indeid." Truly Old Aberdeen was in bad case. As there was no Bishop in the Cathedral, there could be no Chancellor in the University, which was also without either Principal or students. By autumn things had settled down a little; the students returned for the winter session and teaching was resumed, although no Principal had been appointed.

In August, 1640, Dr. Guild was appointed Principal. He, along with Dr. Leslie and the other " Aberdeen Doctors," had refused to sign the Covenant. He had fled to Holland, but returning signed with "reservations." Later still, finding there was a chance of his appointment to the Principalship, he signed the Covenant unreservedly. From a man of this type one could not expect much good, but for the damage he did to the Cathedral his name will always be held in execration. By what spirit he was actuated one cannot say, but one surmises that the damage he wrought to the church was intended to prove his sincerity and zeal for the Covenant. It was not sufficient, however, for he fell under the wrath of the Assembly and was deposed in 1652. He was a great benefactor to the Incorporated Trades of New Aberdeen, probably to spite the town to which he had done so much harm!

The first act of his Principalship was to destroy the Snow Kirk. This little church is seen in Slezer's Map at the foot of the High Street. It was founded by Bishop Elphinstone as the Parish Church of Old Aberdeen in 1497. Its name has given rise to much conjecture, some explaining it by saying that it was peculiarily the church of the fishermen, who went down to the sea in the boats called "snows"; others to the fact that it was dedicated to Santa Maria ad Nives. Principal Guild ordered the masons to "cast down the walls thereof, and to transport the stones to build the College yard dykes and to employ the hewn work to the decayed chamber windows within the College." This aroused great indignation among the people of the Old Town, who resented their parish church being so disgracefully treated. Nothing remains of the church; a small Roman Catholic cemetery is on its site.

The next act of destruction was when Principal Guild, along with the Earl of Seaforth, the Master of Forbes, and the Principal of Edinburgh University, proceeded to St. Machar's Cathedral and ordered "our blessit Lord Jesus Christ, his Armes to be hewen out of the foir front of the pulpit theirof, and to tak down the portrait of our Blissid virgyn Marie and hir deir sone babie Jesus in hir armes, that had stood since the up-putting theirof, in curious wark, under the sylring at the wast end of the pend, quhairon the gryte stepill stands . . . he causit ane mesoun strik out Christe's armes in hewen wark on ilk end of Bishop Gavin Dunbar's tomb; and siklik chissell out the name of Jesus drawin ciphar wayis, I.H.S., out of the tymber wall on the foirsyd of maucher iyll, anent the consistorie dour." The tomb had already suffered at the hand of soldiers who came with the Laird of Auldbar to search the Cathedral vaults for arms.

"The rascall souldieris began to abuse the Bischopis staitlie pallace and spoilzie the same aganes Auldbaris will." It was left to Dr. Guild to complete the destruction. He ordered the fine oak rafters in the great hall of the palace to be cut down and carried to King's College. Spalding truly remarks, "Pitiful to see so glorious a building thus thrown down, first by despitiful soldiers, and then demolished by a Doctor of Divinity." Ten years later what was left of the Bishop's palace was razed to the ground and the stones carried over to New Aberdeen by Cromwell's soldiers, to complete the fortifications on the Castle Hill.

Not content with the mischief he had wrought, in

1642 Principal Guild turned his attention to the Cathedral itself. According to Spalding, he and the minister, Mr. William Strachan, along with William Charles the carpenter, took down the back or reredos of the high altar, which was almost as high as the ceiling. It was considered one of the finest pieces of workmanship in Scotland, and had few equals anywhere. The carpenter, with finer feeling than the Principal and minister, awed probably by the holy place, and very likely actuated by professional admiration for the masterpiece, refused to " put his hand to the downtaking thereof " until the minister should strike the first blow. This Mr. Strachan did, and " syne the wark was begun." It was carried out very clumsily, however. In taking down one of the three great timber crowns at the top, which they were particularly anxious to save, they let it fall upon the ladder, which was broken into three pieces. The crown itself was smashed into a thousand fragments, and even the pavement of the church was broken up.

At Mr. Strachan's instigation a loft or gallery was built across the Cathedral, " quhilk took away the staitly sicht and glorious schaw of the body of the haill kirk." He decorated " the forisyde and baksyde of this beistlie loft with the bak of the altar and other ornaments." His excuse was that there was not sufficient seating accommodation in the church. In order to ensure the regular attendance of the congregation, Mr. Strachan had hit upon the plan of reading from the pulpit the names of all absentees, which, as Spalding allows, " drew such a fair auditory that the seats of the kirk were not able to hold them." All this was done without the knowledge of the Kirk Session. Mr. Strachan then plastered over the part of the church where the back of the altar had been "that it should not be kent."

In spite of the harm he did to the building Mr. Strachan seems to have been much appreciated in Old Aberdeen. He received several calls to go to Edinburgh, but declined them all. In passing judgment on his conduct, we must try to make some allowance for him on account of the very difficult times in which he lived. We are told "he taught powerfullie and plainlie the Word to the gryt comfort of his auditorus."

In the Kirk Session records there are many allusions to the "daskes" or pews of the Trades. For instance, the weavers ask for more room and the tailors ask "for libertie to put a head upon thar dask and for a back pew to be added to their seat." These pews were evidently in the body of the church. At what time lofts or galleries were put up for the Trades I do not know, nor can I find any allusion to their erection in the Kirk Session records. This is not surprising, as so many things which we would certainly have expected to find mentioned are omitted. Not one word is said of the raid upon the Cathedral by Dr. Guild in 1642, nor of the collapse of the Great Tower in 1688, nor of the end of Episcopacy in Scotland in the same year.

Lofts were built, however, and in the beginning of the 19th century there were double rows of galleries on each side of the church, and one at each end. The gallery in the east end was called the college loft, and was reserved for the Principal, professors and students. Over the front of it hung a rich Turkey carpet. The Principal and professors had chairs in front, that of the Principal being more ornamented than the others. The porter and sacrist sat on the right and left of the Principal; the students occupied the seats behind. If all tales are true, their behaviour was not always so exemplary as it might have been. Rumour has it that one Sunday the congregation was electrified by a shout of, "Mon, you're cheatin'; that's my Jock!"

On the north and south aisles were galleries which were occupied by the Trades, with their armorial bearings in front. The Provost and magistrates had a special seat in the south gallery, which, like that of the University, had a handsome Turkey carpet hung over the front. The west gallery was called the "Common Loft."

It is to Mr. Strachan that we owe the appointment of two ministers in the Cathedral as colleagues. In 1648 he pointed out to the Kirk Session that, on account of "the vastness of the paroch and the multitude theirintil it was too gryte ane burding to ane man." We must remember that the Cathedral had to serve an enormous district, a large part of Aberdeen being included in the parish, as well as the country districts on the north. Mr. Strachan suggested either that the parish be divided or a second minister be appointed. This seemed to the Kirk Session to be the better plan, and a Mr. Seaton was appointed to the second charge. Ever since this time the Cathedral has had collegiate ministers. In spite of all that has been written against collegiate charges, and in spite of the very evident difficulties of the position, St. Machar's has been blessed with men who by the exercise of Christian charity and tact have got on well together and have shown their people an example in all good things.

When the collegiate system was adopted, the church was still Episcopal, although no Bishop was appointed from 1638, when Bishop Bellenden was deposed by the Glasgow Assembly, till 1661, when Dr. Mitchell was appointed. He died two years later, and was buried in the Cathedral, his body having lain for one night in St. Ninian's Chapel on the Castle Hill, as was the custom in those days. Dr. Mitchell was followed by Bishop Burnett, who was presented to the See by Charles II. His stay in Old Aberdeen was very short, as he was appointed Archbishop of Glasgow in 1664. His successor was Bishop Scougal, 1664-1682, whose monument in the Cathedral is still very conspicuous, and must have been even more so when the bright colours with which it was ornamented were fresh and new. Where the Bishops lived after their palace was destroyed, I do not know, but evidently from the very short time that any of the later Bishops stayed in Old Aberdeen their position was not a very happy one. We know that some of them at any rate did not receive a penny from the Episcopal revenues; their stipend came to them as parochial clergymen from the magistrates. Professor Henry Scougal, son of the

Bishop, died in the room in the tower at the west end of the church. He is said to have grown so fat that his body had to be lowered from the window. George Haliburton, the last of the Bishops, was appointed by Charles II. in 1682, and held office till 1689, when the Estates abolished Episcopacy.

The Presbyterian ministers who succeeded Mr. Strachan were, many of them, Regents at King's College first and afterwards were appointed to the Cathedral. Of these I may mention Dr. Scroggie, son of a former minister. He had been deprived of his chair in King's College by the General Assembly of 1639. Some years later he was appointed to the first charge of St. Machar's Cathedral, which position he held for a very short time, as two years later he "took sikneis and continued sick untill it pleased the Lord to remove him from hence to Eternitie." He was succeeded by Mr. Middleton, first Regent and then sub-Principal of King's College, which position he lost in 1652 when Gilbert Rule came "into the College by violence and without minding forms." A small compensation was paid to Middleton at the Restoration for his extrusion from the College. He was appointed to St. Machar's in 1661; one year later he left the Cathedral to be Principal of King's College, where he had the distinction of having been "the first Regent that entered in a married condition in this College."

Another interesting man was Mr. George Garden. First a Regent in King's College, he became minister in the Cathedral, from which he went to the Church of St. Nicolas. In 1692 he was deprived of his charge there because of his refusal to pray for Their Majesties, William and Mary. In 1701 the Assembly deposed him for "Bourignianism." I wonder how many ministers of the church could tell us what this is, or was!

We have seen that the University had its own loft or gallery in the Cathedral, to which the Professors and students came every Sunday morning. It must have been a brave sight when the procession left King's College, headed by the Sacrist in his purple gown. The Principal, gowned in black, followed him; then came the Professors, each at the head of his red-gowned class. According to the confession of some of the students, the procession at the Cathedral was not quite so large as when it started from King's College, the lanes of the Old Town offering a means of escape to those at the tail. The election of Principal Chalmers to be minister of St. Machar proves the close connection between the Cathedral and King's College, as the office was to be held in conjunction with that of Principal of the University.

The next great storm which shook the Church was the Disruption of 1843, when "for Conscience Sake" four hundred and seventy-four ministers left the Church of their fathers. Dr. Smith was in the first charge of St. Machar's Cathedral at that time, and I have heard his daughter say that he and his colleague, Dr. Forbes, were the only two ministers in Aberdeen who remained faithful to the Established Church. Between them, she said, they kept all the churches open till appointments could be made. This Dr. Forbes was truly a

" man o' pairts." In addition to being in the second charge of Humanity in King's College he held besides " an appointment to teach a class of Chemistry and Natural History." I wonder if any of the professors of to-day would consider themselves capable of such a multiplicity of duties.

Dr. Smith was succeeded by Dr. Jamieson, who had been in the second charge for twenty years. He was a man of very exceptional gifts; he published many theological works which showed a certain amount almost of genius : the " little more " in his case would have made him a great man. As it is, I am afraid his books are unread, and he is chiefly remembered by his extraordinary sayings in the pulpit and his very curious Scriptural speculations. His appearance was most remarkable, his long, white beard, which reached his waist, giving him a truly patriarchal appearance. His wife was one of the saints on earth, whose like we shall never see again. She had an enormous family, of whom she brought up ten, five sons and five daughters, on a most inadequate income. Dr. Jamieson was succeeded by his colleague, Dr. Calder, who resigned his charge after almost fifty years' work as a minister. Dr. M'Ewen, who succeeded Dr. Calder, served as a territorial soldier all the years of the Great War. On his death in 1923 Dr. MacGilchrist was appointed to the first charge. Two years later Mr. M'Glashan, who had discharged the duties of the second charge with great acceptance to the Cathedral congregation, was appointed minister of Strichen Parish; his place was filled by the Rev.

Melville Dinwiddie, who served in the Gordon Highlanders all through the war, earning the high honours of M.C., O.B.E., D.S.O. On the lamented death of Dr. MacGilchrist in 1928, it was decided by the congregation to abolish the collegiate charge, which, as we have seen, was first instituted in 1648 by Mr. Strachan, and Mr. Dinwiddie was appointed sole minister of the Cathedral.

Before leaving this part of my subject, I think it would be interesting to trace the changes in the sacred Cathedral building itself. Built and adorned by the loving care and generosity of successive Bishops, the internal decorations suffered grievous harm at the hands of the Reformers. The beautiful carved work was thrown out, the gold and silver plate and gorgeous vestments of the clergy were all scattered, lofts that greatly disfigured the church were erected, and to crown all this destruction wrought by man, the great steeple, built by Bishop Elphinstone, fell, destroying the roof of the transepts and part of the roof of the nave. It must have seemed to the terrified people that Providence was taking its share in the work of destruction, but, doubtless, there was a natural reason for the collapse of the tower at this time. One explanation given is, that the soldiers in taking away the stones for the barracks on Castle Hill undermined the steeple; another and more likely explanation is that in 1687 the King's masons found the tower in a bad condition, and workmen were sent to build " buttrages " to strengthen it. They commenced operations by " clearing out at the foundation, instead of building out over from it." The bells were rescued, thanks to the courage of some of the inhabitants, who risked their lives to save them. A subscription to restore the Cathedral was started, and enough money was raised to re-roof the transepts and build a wall across the east end, which must have totally altered the appearance of the interior. The chancel, which apparently had never been finished, had now disappeared altogether, along with the great altar and the many smaller ones. Bishop Dunbar's tomb in the south aisle had been much destroyed; in the beginning of the 18th century the aisle itself was ruined by the stones at the east end being carried off to King's College for some repairs there. Bishop Leighton's tomb on the east side, in St. John's aisle, although it too suffered, showed the Bishop with the mitre on his head and the pastoral staff in his hand. The tomb that has caused the most discussion is one on the wall of the south side of the Cathedral. It shows a full length recumbent figure, draped as a Canon. Below is a slab with an inscription so obliterated that nothing can be made out but the words, "Hic jacet." Tradition, on which I rely so much, says that this monument was erected to the memory of Archdeacon John Barbour, author of "The Brus," who died 13th March, 1395. These along with Bishop Scougal's monument formed the chief ornaments when the Cathedral was opened as the parish church in 1689.

Not for long were the clergy and Kirk Session left in quiet possession, however. A determined attempt was made to reintroduce Episcopacy in 1715, with the return of Prince Charlie. Episcopacy must still have had a very strong hold over the people, as we read in 1714 that Dr. J. Sharp succeeded in "setting up the English service last Lord's Day," the mob having broken open the doors of the church on the Saturday night. Not only that, but the mob took possession of the church and churchyard, not allowing any of the usual congregation to enter. Apparently Dr. Sharp and his friends kept the church for at least two Sundays. When they were at last ejected, Dr. Sharp took away with him "the Church Bible, pulpit and latron green cloathes with there silk fringes, bason and bason cloath and sand-glass." These were all returned some six months later. The next year Mr. Barclay, "sometyme incumbent at Peterhead did by order of the Sheriff intrude and take possession of the church, no access theretoo being allowed to the minister albeit he came at the ordinary tyme at the ringin-in of the third and last bell . . . immediately the minister with the congregation went from the church door to the minister's own house and the minister preached there to the people in the forenoon." In 1716, by desire of the Presbytery of Aberdeen, notice was made from the pulpit of the deposition of six Episcopal clergymen, "late intruders into the parishes of Aberdeen." Two years later the strong partisan feeling is shown in a curious manner. Permission had been given to Mr. William Black, sub-Principal of King's College, to erect a monument opposite his grave in the south aisle of the church, on condition that no inscription should be put on "the said tomb or monument, that any-wayes might reflect on the present Established Church

Government or on any partie or persons whatsoever." On inspection of the tomb the ministers and Kirk Session found "inscriptions on the said tomb which were both dissobligeing and reflecting and therfor the Session do's and hereby do enact that the workemen be stopt from the said work ay and til such time till the said inscription be altered or removed."

The trouble was renewed in 1745, when we read that, "There was no sermon this afternoon because of the troublesome times and the great disturbance given in the Forenoon by some of the Rebels, who came running into the church and calling aloud for their associates." The poor church treasurer suffered badly at this time, as some of the Jacobite soldiers were quartered upon him who "on pain of military execution forced him to give them ten pounds sterling of the Poors' Money." The Session unanimously agreed to make this good. The next year we read that the Synod of Aberdeen had appointed a Fast Day, but, "in regard of the victory obtained by H.R.H. the Duke of Cumberland over the rebels it was thought proper that the day be observed as a day of thanksgiving, and the congregation were exhorted to abstain from their ordinary employments and to spend the day in a religious manner and to attend publick worship at the ordinary time, both Fore and After Noon."

I fear that for those of our generation the services of the Cathedral would not have held any great attraction, and one can hardly wonder that the reaction against the old Scottish Sabbath tends to go too far in the opposite direction. Truly Sunday must have been a day to dread, instead of a day to rejoice in, as was meant. Strict rules were laid down by the Kirk Session, supported by the Town Council, that every person should attend divine service; an elder and a town's officer were appointed to go through the whole town, from the Spital to the Bridge of Don, to make note of any who should be found absent from church. Not only so, but once in church there was no escape till after the benediction was pronounced, which was sometimes not till the end of the afternoon service! An elder stood at the door to prevent any backsliders slipping out. Once safely in church, no one was allowed to make a custom of sleeping, but if sleep proved too much for him he was "not to take evil with it if anyone wakened him." Farmers were not even allowed the solace of the company of their dogs; to bring dogs to church was strictly forbidden.

Even when the service ended in the forenoon, the people had to go straight to their own homes and there, behind drawn blinds, spend Sunday afternoon "praying, conferring and singing psalms." In spite of this, or because of it, much of the time of the Kirk Session was taken up judging cases of Sabbath breaking. Human nature was too strong in fallen man, who persisted in fishing, playing bowls or golf, driving sheep, and even in one case "driving naked swine in the College Bounds" on a Sunday. The guilty persons were punished by having to make public repentance or pay a fine. Truly, looking back, one can sympathise with those weaker brethren who cut adrift altogether; and yet does the Scottish character not owe a great deal of its dour independence to the hard training of those long-gone-bye years? I cannot help dreading that in our anxiety to give the young people a good time we are bringing up a race which will not find it easy to keep up the good old Scottish traditions.

The Sunday service itself must have been very dull to those whose ancestors had been Roman Catholics and who themselves had been accustomed to the brighter form of Episcopalian worship. We can picture our forefathers sitting on hard wooden pews, in a church bare of all ornament, with whitewashed walls and pillars! The sermons, delivered from a pulpit very unlike Bishop Stewart's beautiful carved one, were doubtless occupied with the theological problems which appealed so strongly to the Scot of a hundred years ago. As very few of the congregation had books, the singing of the psalms was a matter of difficulty. Yet the congregation is ordered to sing! or, if that is impossible for them, "they must give good attention to those who can." The absence of books was got over by the minister or precentor reading out each line separately, which was then sung by the congregation. By the end of the 18th century it was resolved to discontinue this custom, and the congregation were recommended to provide themselves with psalm books, and to get by heart the psalms that were most frequently sung. Excellent advice! Till the end of the 19th century, however, the practice of reading the psalm line by line before singing it was continued on Communion Sundays, when the precentor read out the lines of the 103rd Psalm, which were sung by the choir and the congregation dispersing by the east door from the first Communion Table. The psalms were sung sitting; the congregation stood for prayer — a very tiring business, as some of the prayers lasted for about twenty minutes. This custom was given up in the Cathedral when Dr. Jamieson announced in his characteristic manner that the Kirk Session had decided that the congregation should in future stand to sing and for prayer "adopt the reverent attitude, heads downwards"!

Before leaving this part of my subject, I must allude shortly to some pronouncements of the Kirk Session which throw side-lights upon the times in which our ancestors lived. It is interesting to find that Old Aberdeen possessed warlocks and witches. In 1633 a man was absolved from having raised the wind that blew down the College Crown, while another had to stand in sackcloth for the sin of "charming." Charming, in order to cure disease, is, we are told particularly, forbidden by the Word of God, but it seems to have been a lucrative trade all the same. A woman was accused of having "clasped a calf in her arms which therefter did wannishe," and not only that but she "came over the watter of Don without ane boat."

Merrymaking at weddings was strictly forbidden; the number of guests was, according to Act of Parliament, limited to eight, while drinking at lyke wakes was also strongly condemned.

The Kirk Session showed a great interest in the

children of the parish. They visited the school regularly, and exhorted parents to "put ther chyldren to scooles that they might be instructed to read that the familie worship might be promowed bot in towne and parisch and that everie familie might have one at least within it that might read." The Session also had some regard for the safety of the children, who had been in the habit of playing in the steeple and ceiling of the church. It orders the "beddalls in time coming to prevent the like for the future." So long ago as 1758 the Session took into their serious consideration the very great danger that mothers and infants ran from being attended by midwives not qualified for their profession, and recommended that the elders of the various districts should draw the attention of the people to this and to the encouragement and assistance that the Kirk Session was willing to give to any suitable young woman who will go through a proper training. When we remember that this subject is still under consideration in the year 1928, we can pride ourselves on the wisdom and foresight of the elders of 1758.

How the Cathedral was lit in the early days of Presbyterianism I cannot imagine. Doubtless afternoon service began very early, and it would probably be over soon after three o'clock, but even so I should think that in the depths of winter candles must, in spite of their Romish aroma, have been necessary in the pulpit. Gas, which had been introduced into Aberdeen early in the 19th century, was brought into the Cathedral during the improvements of 1867. Old pictures show us the pews supporting an upright stalk with arms on either side carrying the gas. There were great objections to this manner of lighting, and another plan was hit upon during the ill-omened improvements in the end of the century. Ornamental metal rings carrying the gas pipes were fastened round our beautiful pillars, a piece of vandalism which yet was much admired! The introduction of electric light was an extraordinary improvement. The work was done most artistically, and the result has been all that one could hope for.

After the Disruption of 1843 the Cathedral congregation was much reduced in numbers. Several quoad sacra churches had been built in the parish, King's College Chapel had been re-opened for worship, so that the members of the University no longer required their gallery in the Cathedral, and a church had been built in Old Aberdeen for the members of the new Free Church of Scotland. Under these altered conditions it was found that the galleries were no longer needed; they were taken down, and at the same time the pillars were cleared of the disfiguring whitewash.

Doubtless one of the houses belonging to the clergy of the Roman Catholic Church had been given to the minister of the Cathedral as his manse. So early as 1647 reference is made to his glebe; three years later the Session decided that a manse or glebe should be given to the second minister. When he lost this I do not know, but certainly there was no manse for the minister of the second charge till 1878, when funds were raised and a manse built. A great effort was made about this time to restore the Cathedral and make it more like what it had been in the days of its greatness. The scheme had to be abandoned on account of the enormous cost and the impossibility of making such a church suitable for the requirements of Presbyterian worship. The wall at the east end of the church, which contained a large door under a fine old window, was replaced by the present very large window, which is not of such a fine design as the old one. The organ which was introduced at this time appears to have been the first in the Cathedral. Great difficulty was found in choosing a site for it. The original intention was to build it in two parts, one on either side of the church, between the pillars. So many objections were raised by those who possessed graves or vaults in the Cathedral that after much discussion it was resolved to build the organ in front of the east window and place the pulpit immediately in front of it. It was seen at once that the result was worse even than had been dreaded; but what could be done? Much money had been spent; the congregation could not be expected to contribute to undo what had just been done. There was nothing for it but to wait till a reasonable time had elapsed and then make a fresh effort. Thanks to the courage and faith of the Rev. Dr. MacGilchrist and the Rev. Melville Dinwiddie, a scheme has been carried through which has given the congregation and the people of Aberdeen a Cathedral worthy of its great tradition and history.

The organ, which is a truly magnificent instrument,

St. Machar's Cathedral Interior, 1929.

has been removed to the side, the walls have been stripped of their disfiguring plaster, and the Cathedral now looks more like its ancient self than it has done since the troubles came upon it.

KING'S COLLEGE AND UNIVERSITY

WILLIAM ELPHINSTONE was appointed to the charge of St. Machar Cathedral and Diocese in 1483. Born and educated in Glasgow, he took his Master's Degree in Arts at the age of twenty-five, after which he was ordained priest. From his very early years it was borne in upon him that he was called in a special manner to serve the Virgin Mary. Some four years after his graduation he went to the University of Paris to prepare himself for public life. His zeal for work and his ability soon made themselves evident; he was appointed First Reader of Canon Law, a very distinguished office. He was frequently consulted by the Parliament of Paris, and gained the friendship of some of the most learned and best known men of the time. Recalled to Glasgow, he was appointed Dean of the Faculty of Arts and Rector of the University. James III., requiring an Ambassador to the Court of France of Louis the Eleventh, made choice of Elphinstone, and on his return to Scotland offered him the Bishopric of Ross. Shortly afterwards the charge of St. Machar's Cathedral fell vacant and was offered to Elphinstone. As the Cathedral was dedicated to the Virgin, Elphinstone felt that here was the work for which he had been intended, and that in Old Aberdeen he would find the sphere for which he had been destined.

In Old Aberdeen there was a College of Canons, founded by Malcolm IV., about whose origin many tales are told, some writers even claiming for it the position of a University. Orem speaks of it as "a Studium generale where there were professors and doctors of divinity and many learned men have flourished therein." The existence of such an institution may have suggested to Bishop Elphinstone the possibility of founding a University in Old Aberdeen, and so emulating his brother bishops, Henry Wardlaw, who founded the University of St. Andrews in 1411, and Bishop Turnbull, who founded Glasgow University some forty years later. The extreme desirability of a University in a Cathedral town must have been very apparent to a man like Elphinstone, thoroughly imbued with the University spirit from his long connection with the Universities of Glasgow and Paris.

His appointment to the Chancellorship of Scotland in 1488 gave him the chance of enlisting the sympathy and help of James IV., who wrote to His Holiness the Pope, Alexander VI., asking his authority for the erection of a University in Old Aberdeen, giving as his reasons the benighted condition and profound ignorance of the inhabitants, and claiming for Aberdeen a very salubrious and mild climate. The result of this appeal was a Bull, dated 10th February, 1494, instituting a University in Old Aberdeen. The Bull is preserved in King's College Library, the "Bulla" or seals being still in excellent condition. The plans for the University included the Faculties of Theology, Canon and Civil Law, Arts and Medicine.

Bishop Elphinstone, Bishop of the Diocese, constituted himself and his successors in office Chancellors of the University. In this way the Church was head not only of matters religious and secular but of matters educational.

The College was dedicated to the Virgin, and was called "Sancta Maria in Nativitate." It consisted of thirty-six members—namely, a Doctor of Theology, who was also the Principal; a Doctor of Civil Law, a Doctor of Canon Law, a Doctor of Physic, a Professor of Humanity to teach Grammar, a sub-Principal to teach Philosophy, a Cantor, a Sacrist, six students in Divinity, three students in Law, thirteen students in Philosophy, an Organist, and five singing boys who were students in Humanity. The Principal, Canonist, Civilist, Mediciner, sub-Principal, and Grammarian were all nominated by the Chancellor. The Rector was chosen by the votes of all the members of the University, who gave their votes in "nations" according to their birthplace. In this arrangement we see very clearly the influence exerted upon Elphinstone by the University of Paris, where the students, drawn from all over the world, gave their votes for a procurator to act for each nation in the choice of a Rector. This ancient custom is still followed in the Universities of Aberdeen and Glasgow.

It is quite clear that the University of Old Aberdeen was open to students before any attempt was made to erect buildings. The necessity for these was proved by the success which attended the early years of the University, and we know from the inscription near the west door of King's College Chapel that "masons began to build in 1500." The Charter of Bishop Elphinstone containing the first foundation of the College, written immediately after the completion of the buildings, is dated 1505.

Hector Boece, Lecturer on Philosophy in Paris, was chosen by Elphinstone as the Principal of the new University. He arrived in Old Aberdeen in the spring of 1500. One cannot help wondering what his feelings were when he found himself in this "grey, wintry-featured sea-throned Aberdeen." Did he ever regret Paris, that gay, beautiful city, with its University attended by 10,000 students from all countries? It cannot have been the lure of money that tempted him to come, for his salary was only forty Scottish merks, or about £30! Love of his friend William Elphinstone, love of Scotland, and the love of adventure all may have had something to do with his decision, which was a happy one for the new University. His position was much better than it seems on the face of it, for in addition to his salary he held a Canon's Stall and the Rectorship of Tyrie.

By 1505 the buildings, including the chapel, were finished. Of it we have the following description by Boece—

"he builds
A statlie structure there,
A fabric firm and fair,
Which has a temple tabulate
Of polished stones and squair.
With tables, celrings, seats,

At the south-east corner of the hall stood the ivy tower; behind the hall were the quarters of the Œconomus and the well from which water was drawn for the University. In the well lived an eel, fabulously old.

Such then was King's College as built by Bishop Elphinstone in 1505. Not for long was he to rejoice in the work of his hands. Troubles came thick and fast upon Scotland. It is said that after the fatal field of Flodden Elphinstone was never seen to smile. He died in 1514, and his body was laid to rest in the College Chapel. A plain black marble slab is all that is left of a very ornate tomb, of which a full account is given in the Inventory in King's College Library. Over the stone were eight figures in brass, representing the four cardinal virtues, the three Christian graces and contemplation. Two angels holding candelabra over the head and two attendants at the feet bearing an epitaph in brass surmounted the recumbent figure of the Bishop clad in his pontifical robes. A few years ago an attempt was made by some of Bishop Elphinstone's admirers to restore the tomb to something like its pristine glory. The result of their endeavours—a very marvellous piece of statuary—may be seen in the Anti-Chapel. Unfortunately, it is far too large and heavy for Elphinstone's beautiful little chapel. In itself it is truly a work of art, and one must sympathise with those whose wish to honour the memory of one of Scotland's greatest men should have been frustrated by the zeal of the artist.

It was to Bishop Gavin Dunbar that we owe the

original tomb. On him fell the duty of carrying on Elphinstone's plans, not only for the University but also for the Cathedral and the Bridge of Dee. He finished King's College tower with a legacy left by Elphinstone for the purpose. "Above a double arche crossed of stone there standeth a crown royall, octangular, supported with eight pillars, the top of the crown a stone globe—above it a double crosse gilded, intimating that it is the King's College." In the tower were the bells given to the University by Elphinstone. We are told that two of them were the largest in Scotland, and that their harmony was such that they might call the very stones to prayer. The bells were named Trinitas, Maria, Micael, Gabriel and Raphael.

Bishop Dunbar died in 1532, and Boece, the first Principal of the University, in 1536. Dunbar's tomb is in the Cathedral, but Boece was buried in the chapel, close to Elphinstone. Bishop Stewart, who succeeded, gave to the Cathedral the carved pulpit which is used in the chapel to-day. Principal Hay succeeded Boece. So far as we know, the great event of his principalship was a visit in 1541 of King James V. and Queen Mary. They were the guests of the Bishop, but lived at King's College in the apartments of the Principal, which were "two, entered by ane portal door of aik carved work. They had ane gret stand and bed of aik ceiled and hung about with three curtains, reid worsat and green, and ane fedder bed with bowstar." Royalty must have been easily housed in these days, but much trouble and expense were taken to suitably entertain the King and Queen in which, no doubt, the famous "fule" of Aberdeen took part. "Divers triumphs and plays were arranged by the town and city, the university and schools thereof, exercises and disputations, orations in Greek, Latin and other languages, quhilk was mickle commended be the King and Queen and all their Companie." This mention of Greek is interesting, as the date generally given for its introduction into Scotland is 1534. We probably owe it to Elphinstone, Boece and Hay and their training in Paris that King's College was so far ahead of the times.

Under Bishop Stewart it was found necessary to increase the accommodation at the University. Buildings consisting of a chapter and jewel house, and a classroom with a library above it, were built against the wall of the Chapel. Very strict rules had been laid down by Elphinstone for the discipline of the University. Residence and the wearing of gowns and caps were compulsory; any student neglecting this rule in hall, classes or chapel was deprived of his meals. Bursars wore black gowns, other students red.

Meals were supplied in the hall by the Œconomus and his wife, who was the only woman allowed to cross the threshold of King's College. The wages of the Œconomus were paid partly in money and partly in kind.

By the middle of the 16th century the storm which had long been brewing in the Church manifested itself in the lax discipline of the University. Elphinstone had provided a system of visitations to deal with the possibility of such an event. In 1549 the Rector,

Galloway of Kinkell, ordered a visitation—the second of which we have a record. Galloway was accompanied by the Archdeacon of Aberdeen and by three Canons of the Cathedral. They enjoined amendment, drew up a plan of life for professors and scholars, and commanded the Principal and sub-Principal to preach at least seven times a year. It was all in vain—the outside forces were too strong and the turmoil in the country was inevitably reflected in the universities as in the church. Aberdeen, it is well known, kept comparatively calm. The nobles were Royalists and supporters of the Church, and the people were not keen "Reformers." The full effect of the storm was not felt till 1560, when Alexander Anderson was Principal. Knox says of him that "he was more subtle and crafty than either learned or godly," but he had the great virtue of the courage of his convictions. He absolutely refused to profess the Reformed Faith, although it meant the loss of his position. His physical courage also was not lacking, for we read of him defending the college gate in person against the attack of a rascally multitude headed by the Barons of the Mearns, come with the intention of carrying away the lead from the college roof, as well as Elphinstone's famous bells.

Anderson was the last Roman Catholic Principal. Seventy-five years after its foundation, Elphinstone's University, dedicated to the Virgin and named by him the University of St. Mary's, passed into the control of the Presbyterian Church. It may be well to notice here that the name King's College was never formally given to the University. It seems to have slipped gradually into popular use and become firmly established.

The first Protestant Principal, in 1569, was Alexander Arbuthnot. King's College was as fortunate in its first post-Reformation Principal as it had been in the famous scholar whom Elphinstone brought from Paris. The Reformation, however, brought about a great change in the Scottish University system in that it could no longer be part of one grand European community. Professor Rait says, "The old conception of a University could not survive the triumph of the New Faith." Many foreign students had been attracted to the Scottish Universities. Ferrerius, writing in 1534, says that Aberdeen was the most famous of them all. After the Reformation these visits ceased.

Arbuthnot and Andrew Melville, Principal of Glasgow University, drew up a "nova fundatio" for Aberdeen, as had been done by the other Scottish Universities, to adapt them to the change of Church government. This was approved by the Assembly of 1583. It was, however, bitterly opposed by some of the members of King's College, whose duties and emoluments it swept away. They appealed to the King, who put his veto on the resolution of the Assembly.

We have seen that during the struggle between Prelacy and Presbyterianism the sympathies of King's College were with the Royal prerogative and the modified Episcopacy which it established. This fact led to the foundation of Marischal College in Aberdeen, which is another story.

We can quite well understand that great tact and skill must have been necessary to guide the University in these very troublous times, and we need not be surprised that Bishop Patrick Forbes on his accession to the Episcopal See in 1618 found a great lack of discipline in the University. His interest in it was so great that he has been called its "second founder." He obtained from King Charles a Commission giving him authority to inquire into its order and discipline. He found that there was in the college "lamentable heathenism and sic lowness as is horrible to record." The treasury was empty and of the silver spoons given by the graduates not one remained. His zeal and vigilance did much, however. He re-established divine service in the chapel, where his chair may still be seen, he improved the teaching, and through his influence a printing press was set up.

The rivalry between the University of Aberdeen and its older sister had become so bitter, and the whole situation of two Universities, each granting degrees in the same subjects within a mile of one another, was so anomalous that King Charles resolved to form a union, which he called the Caroline University. This union was purely nominal, and lasted for twenty years only.

Aberdeen had been treated fairly leniently till now in matters of conscience, but in 1657 General Monk arrived in the name of Cromwell. His first act was to get rid of William Guild, Principal of King's College, a man who had sat on the fence while the famous

" Aberdeen Doctors " fought for liberty of conscience. As a revenge for being turned out of the Principalship, Guild destroyed the chapel organ, saying that it had on it " a portrait of a woman, naebody kens wha, quhilk is a thing most intolerable in the kirk of a college."

John Row was appointed Principal by Cromwell. Under him the University throve so much that more accommodation was needed. To General Monk we owe the building called Cromwell's Tower, at the north-east corner of the quadrangle. Originally it consisted of six stories, including a billiard room.

A short account of the life led by the students at King's College in Principal Row's time may be interesting. Morning prayers were read at six in summer and six-thirty in winter, after breakfast! Then followed private study till ten, when the roll was called; this was followed by an hour's reading of Scripture. At eleven the Regents revised the morning's work. During dinner, which was at twelve, selections from sacred or secular history were read aloud by one of the bursars. At two p.m. the roll was again called; on three afternoons in the week excursions were made to the links for recreation; on the other afternoons the Principal delivered an address on Hebrew or on Theology. From five till six the students read by themselves, after which supper was served and the students retired to their own rooms to work. All fires and lights had to be out by eleven o'clock—late enough, one would think, considering the early hour of breakfast. To prevent any accident or misdemeanour, a bell was rung at 2 a.m., after which a solemn visitation of the rooms and passages was made. The rules as to behaviour during meals seem strange to us; for instance, students were forbidden to throw bones at each other, but might leave them on their plates or on the floor. The food in those early days consisted of "quhyte breid, ait breid, best aill, secunde aill, beif, muton, smal fische, buttyre, eggis, partens, beir, vinager, peittis, spyse, salt beif, guiss, hennis, fresh hadocks, milk, cheese and skait."

The subjects taught were Greek, Philosophy, Humanity, French, Book-keeping, Writing and Dancing. It is interesting to notice the appointment of the Mediciner before any of the other universities had contemplated teaching Medicine.

The coming of William of Orange immensely stimulated education, and its effects were felt as far North as Aberdeen. The number of students had increased to about seventy, who were famous under Principal Row for their "disputations" in Philosophy, held not in the vernacular but in Greek, Latin, French or English.

Parliament passed an Act in 1690 declaring that every Principal, Professor and Regent must subscribe the Confession of Faith, take the Oath of Allegiance, and acknowledge the Presbyterian Government of the Church. All the officials of King's College, with one exception, subscribed "with mental reservations." In 1715 "mental reservations" gained the day; three professors of King's and six of Marischal were deprived of their offices for joining in a demonstration which proclaimed James VIII. King at the Cross of Old Aberdeen. This Act marks the transfer of the Scottish University from the Church to the Crown.

In 1720 the library, which was built, as we have seen, against the chapel wall, was in a very bad condition. A graduate, Dr. Fraser of Chelsea, most generously came forward with funds for a restoration. The old buildings were taken down, new classrooms were built on the ground floor, and a new library, nearly double the length of the old one, was erected. According to Dr. Macpherson, this library was burned in 1760. The Senatus minutes give no record of this, but in 1773 the professors decided to use the west end of the chapel as a library and to employ the materials from Fraser's building for manses for the professors. The manses of Greek and Mathematics were built at this time.

Soon after this the chapel, which had been used only for graduation ceremonies, was opened for regular Sunday services. From 1683-1823 the University professors and students alike worshipped in the Cathedral. The interior of the chapel was altered to make it suitable for Presbyterian worship; the altar steps were destroyed, and long benches for the students were fitted up. A plaster screen on top of the carved door divided the chapel from the library. Some pictures hung upon this screen, representing scriptural subjects, which were rescued from the old hall by the sacrist, who had them varnished and hung in the chapel as a surprise for the Senatus! They are said to be the work of Jamesone, but are more likely by some of his pupils.

At the restoration of 1890, the organ, for which funds were collected by Professor Milligan, Secretary of the Senatus, was erected above the screen, where the organ destroyed by Principal Guild had formerly stood. At this time, too, the beautiful ceiling of carved oak as well as the walls were painted and the floor re-laid. The artistic taste of one generation is never the same as that of its successor, and many would gladly see unplastered walls and a plain roof.

The behaviour at graduation ceremonies in the chapel was most discreditable, especially when one remembers the nature of the place in which they were held. It is a strange tradition that graduations should always be accompanied by a licence permitted by the student himself at no other time. The chapel is sometimes said to have been the scene of the much-discussed Downie trial and tragedy. To anyone not conversant with this story I would strongly recommend "Life at a Northern University," by Neil M'Lean. Many of the older inhabitants will remember the shouts of the children in the Spital when they saw the red-gowned students "airt and pairt in Downie's slaughter" and the rhyme—

> "They took a man and killed him deid
> And stappit him in a holie,
> Buttery Wullie, Buttery Wullie, Buttery Wullie
> Coley."

Buttery Wullie is said to be derived from the "Collegium Butterense " held in a tavern kept by a Peter Butter.

About the end of the 18th century the students complained of the food supplied to them. At this time there were two tables—those who could afford to pay a little extra sat at the first table. After receiving the bill of fare supplied to the students at St. Andrews, which the professors found to be dearer and not so good as at Aberdeen, they resolved to teach the students a lesson, and substituted for the Sunday roast boiled beef and broth, " which is better for the student and easier for the Œconomus." Breakfast and supper consisted of " half a scone of oat bread with a mutchkin of milk at each diet each day." Dinner was more varied; on Sundays it consisted of eggs, potatoes, bread and butter, along with a scone of oat bread and a mutchkin of ale, which accompanied every dinner except that on Friday. On Mondays, Tuesdays, and Wednesdays beef and broth; Thursdays boiled turnips chopped, with butter and milk; and on Fridays fresh fish with a mutchkin and a half of ale.

In the beginning of the 19th century the residential system had to be abolished. Cheap as it was, lodgings were cheaper, and many of the country lads were supplied with oatmeal, etc., from home. With the decay of the residential system, however, and the loss of professorial supervision, the manners of the students degenerated greatly. As Principal M'Leod said, "They were unco bad examples of economy." Most of them lived in lodgings in the Old Town, where merry pranks were carried on. One mania was to collect door handles, knockers and bell handles, of which some of the students were said to have had a very fine collection.

The number of students had risen enormously, both in King's and Marischal Colleges, and the curriculum had been greatly enlarged. The Government commissioners had for long attempted to draw up a scheme of union between the two Universities. This was successfully carried out in 1858 when it was decided to retain Arts and Divinity at King's College and Law and Medicine at Marischal. The Principal of King's College, the Rev. Dr. Campbell, became Principal of the united University; the office of sub-Principal was abolished and six new Chairs were created.

New classrooms and a library were built at King's; the old dormitories and professorial residences were pulled down to make way for the classrooms, and with the dormitories disappeared the old cloisters which were, Sir William Geddes said, "the sacred spot connected with the college." Later University Commissions have transformed the Faculty of Arts beyond recognition, and have created a new Faculty, that of Science. Women are now admitted freely to all Faculties.

Till the 19th century the student had no place in the government of the University. Elphinstone had decreed that the Rector should be appointed by the students, but not till 1858 was this really done. Till then the professors chose the Rector, much to the indignation of the students, who gave vent to their wrath in squibs and lampoons. The first University magazine, if one may call it so, appeared in MSS. in 1709, full of jeering allusions to the professors. The Aberdeen University Magazine appeared in 1836; it had two successors before *Alma Mater,* which first appeared in 1883.

By far the most useful mouthpiece of democratic feeling among the students and that which keeps them most in touch with the governing body is the Students' Representative Council, the idea of which came from France, and which has proved of great value to the Senatus as well as to the students.

The life led by the student of to-day is naturally something very different from that visualised by Elphinstone, but his University has grown to be something much greater than he had ever dreamed of. Its graduates all over the world uphold its reputation right nobly, and while looking back with loving memories on the good old days spent in the shadow of King's College tower, keep in their hearts its motto—

"Initium Sapientiae, Timor Domini."